D1606285

Zubeida Jaffer

Our Generation

Kwela Books

Kwela Books
40 Heerengracht, Cape Town 8001;
P.O. Box 6525, Roggebaai 8012
kwela@kwela.com

Cover photograph by Rashid Lombard
Book design by Nazli Jacobs
Set in Photina
Printed and bound by Paarl Print,
Oosterland Street, Paarl, South Africa
First edition, third printing 2005

ISBN 0-7957-0148-9

Dedicated to my parents
Raghmat and Hassan Jaffer
On whose backs I stand

Be gentle gentle on my mind
please do be gentle,
soft;
do not crowd my mind
with studied images of my past;
let me feel it first:
do not display my carved rituals
at the British Museum,
for little do they say;
let me feel them first.

It is the fairy tale in me,
the story book
that is the pure tale of my being.
Do go gentle on my mind,
softly please,
soft.

NJABULO NDEBELE

CHAPTER ONE

The pains shoot through my lower back at regular intervals. I have been in labour all night and am starting to grip onto the steel frame of the hospital bed.

The wind howls as it forces its way up against the walls of the maternity hospital just below Signal Hill.

I wait for the rain to come, to break open those heavy clouds that hang over the hill, so that the wind might subside, so that it will stop beating so wildly against the mountain-side, so that my child can come into a world that is cleansed, calm and sweet.

Soon I will know whether we have survived. Whether all her fingers are intact, whether she is deformed in any way. He had intended to kill her. I close my eyes and see him. The security policeman with the red, liquor-bloated face. He is leaning over me. He had just discovered that I was pregnant, days after my arrest.

"Ja, Zubeida, vir my maak dit geen verskil nie." (Yes, Zubeida, to me it makes no difference.)

"Tell us why they were sewing those flags. We will let you go. I promise you."

I see him shifting right up against me, leaning his sweating body against my shoulder, whispering swear words into my ear, insulting me.

I focus my eyes on the Qur'ān on my lap, trying to blot out what he is saying. I am quiet, determined not to answer his questions.

At last I say: "I have nothing to say to you. Nothing."

His face contorts, goes an even deeper red. Drops of perspiration enlarge on his forehead, heated body against my arm.

"As jy dink jy kan hier sit en daardie boek lees, gaan ek dit stukkend smyt teen die muur. Dis nie jou reg nie, ek het dit maar toegelaat." (If you think you can sit here and read that book, I will take it and smash it against that wall. It is not your right, I am just allowing you to have it here.)

I think of my baby. I think of her constantly as the panic rises rapidly in me. He would have to do his damnedest. I am not going to give in to him. Not after what they did to me five years ago. They had drugged the food they served me, stimulating a reaction that took me to the edge of my life. I was barely twenty-two years old, six months into my newspaper career when I was detained and tortured. I know now what is the realm of the possible.

But what if the strain is too much? What if I lose my baby or harm her? Would I be able to have another child?

He continues his tirade in Afrikaans. The threats intensify. "You can forget about seeing your husband alive again. He is taking little tablets already because he cannot stand it. We are making plans so that he will hang himself in his cell," he says and laughs.

"I will personally come and tell you about his death."

This child in me is our child and I want her. I will not see him again. I have to have his child.

Frans Mostert has a terrible reputation. He is not the one who tortured me during my first detention. Then it was my misfortune to land up in the clutches of the notorious Spyker van Wyk. Spyker. Responsible for the death of our imām in 1969. I will never forget my dad's eyes that morning when I first saw Spyker. I woke up to find my dad bending over me. "Beida, the security police are here. You have to get up."

Despite being half-asleep, I was dismissive. "Don't worry, dad, I will speak with them," I said as I sat up, swung my legs from under the blankets and slipped my feet into my sandals. For months, I had covered the uprisings in Cape Town, running from one scene of resistance to another on what felt like a constantly moving escalator. Something in my father's eyes wedged a doubt into my easy confidence, making me ask: "Who is inside, dad?"

His brown eyes looked greenish hazel as his pupils shrank, becoming for me a red stop light. He spoke softly in his fright: "It's Spyker van Wyk himself, Beida."

Beady black eyes, white mat face, black hair oiled down flat on either side of a path running down the middle of his head. Hitler without a moustache. In our living room. This man I had never seen. Responsible for the death of our imām.

By the mid-eighties, in Cape Town and the whole of the Western Cape, Mostert had become the re-incarnation of Spyker. I sit there, considering. I do not doubt that he is capable of cruelty. I have seen it all before. Those men who had drugged and beaten me five years earlier were dentists who had pulled answers from my mouth without administering anaesthesia. Abruptly wiping away my god-given bubbliness, my spontaneous joy of life.

10

At last it comes.

Not only am I a woman but a pregnant woman, and he is going to use this to his advantage.

"You have nothing to say now but I will give you something to help you along. I know just what I am going to do to you. I have prepared a chemical for you to drink if you do not want to cooperate."

He smirks. "You know what that will do to your baby? It will kill it. It will burn your baby from your body."

I sit impassively, not wanting to believe what I have just heard. Would he seriously do this? Yes he could. No he would not. Yes he would. During my last detention, they had drugged me.

Yes, he would do it. I see it in his face. Triumphant, he turns and walks from the cell, all his tension drained, relaxed, confident that when he comes back, I will comply.

The door of the delivery ward swings open, breaking my reverie. I watch the nurse draw the curtains around the bed next to me. The door opens again and they wheel in another expectant mother. She moans, then shouts: "Liewe Here!" (Dearest God.) They wheel her to the bed. I cannot see. The curtains obstruct my view. She wails.

"Shu, mummy. Shu," says the nurse.

Silence for a minute. Then she screams. How many more women will they wheel in tonight while I lie here? It's close to midnight now and I have been in labour since about 8 p.m.

The door swings open again. I look up expectantly, ready to smile. It must be him. I have been waiting for hours now. It cannot be long before my husband joins me. We have made elaborate arrangements so that he can be with me. A friend brought me to the hospital with great secrecy to prevent the police from knowing that I had gone into labour. We had told no-one except the doctor.

Two weeks earlier, the government had imposed a state of emergency. The security police had swooped down on thousands of activists around the country to prevent them from organising the popular resistance. They were hunting my husband and had forced me to leave our home twice since the start of the emergency.

Just this morning, I trudged with my big belly into the trade union offices where I work to witness the damage they have done.

Yesterday they came with casspirs and machine guns and surrounded the office in Woodstock. This was largely a consequence of them having placed Cape Underwear, a clothing factory, under siege in Epping. They had arrived at the factory as we were holding a secret ballot to determine worker support for a new union. Only seventy-seven of the nearly four hundred workers had ventured to vote as they watched the heavily armed men station themselves outside the factory. Forty-four had voted for the Clothing Workers Union and thirty-three for the old Garment Workers Union we were opposing.

After leaving the factory, the armed men had headed for Woodstock, where they had arrested all the organisers present in the office. Three of the six arrested were workers suspended from the factory as a result of an ongoing dispute.

This morning I found everything in a shambles – documents strewn across the floor, desks overturned and the printing presses smashed. My baby was pressing down on my bladder, bringing the first symptoms of labour.

Nazier Seria, a sympathetic architect who had helped plan our offices, was there. He kindly helped me into his car and took me to the doctor.

"We must book you in, Zubeida," said Dr Aziz Samie. "You are dilating."

"I can't go now," I said. "They arrested all our organisers yesterday and I have to go for help. As soon as I am done, I will go straight to St. Monica's."

As I wait at the hospital now, watching the door, I relive every moment of the morning, Nazier and I speeding to Athlone to the office of Essa Moosa where most of us landed up at some time or another. Essa Moosa is a small man with a big heart. When we get there he instructs his attorney, Bashir Waglay, to bring an interdict to secure the release of those detained. The families have to be brought together for a meeting and I get onto the telephone. By the middle of the day, I have spoken to all the relevant family members and arranged for them to meet at Essa's office at 6 p.m. I finally call Nazier and ask if he will run the meeting. He agrees. I find a friend to take me about ten streets away.

"Just drop me here," I say. I have to walk to get to where my husband is. It's about two kilometres away. My husband is in hiding and we never ever allow anybody near where he lives. It is safer that way for them. So it is always having to walk in a convoluted way. Never a straight line. Always a zig-zag, to make sure that no-one is following. This afternoon, the task is arduous. I can feel that my huge belly is hanging low as I will my legs and arms to move me down the road, at all times looking over my shoulder. I

12

sink into the couch when I arrive at the house and say nothing. I do not have to. He can see that I am finished, a moribund patient in desperate need of care.

"You just relax," he says, hunching up his strong muscular shoulders as he bends over me to place a cushion under my head. "I will sort out all the arrangements to get you to the hospital."

Of course it is not so easy. He could not just pick up the telephone and make a call, without alerting police to his whereabouts. He has to find somebody to find somebody else to find the person he wants who has agreed to help. So it takes a good few hours before everything is in place. When I finally settle my tired body onto the crispy white bed-sheets of St Monica's, it is 8 p.m. and the labour has started.

And here I am, hours later, eyes on the swinging door. I have once again readied my smile unnecessarily. A stranger steps into the ward and scans the beds for his wife. He confers with the nurse and then walks towards the far end of the ward to the last bed. The cries and shouts in the bed next to me have subsided. The baby has been born, carried away to the nursery and the mother is sleeping. By nature, I am not one to shout and perform. I have inherited the family trait that we consider a strength and a weakness – a quiet stoïcism when faced with crises. The hysteria usually comes later, or lodges in our bodies, bringing on some physical illness. But shouting, crying and screaming? Oh no! We are too polite for that.

The pain grips my lower abdomen. I gasp. "Nurse," I whisper hoarsely. She moves across from the far side of the ward. "Yes, mummy?"

"Nurse, I want an epidural."

"An epidural!" The conversation is in Afrikaans. "Jy kan nie nou vra vir 'n epidural nie." (You cannot ask for an epidural now.)

"But nurse, the doctor said I could ask if it all became too much."

"Not now," she says.

I can see this one is not going to be very helpful. Why, if modern science has made advances to save women from the pain of birth, must I be subjecting myself to this? After about nine hours in labour, I am beginning to change my mind about the joys of natural birth. I summon all the energy I can to give my voice some authority. "Nurse, the doctor said I could get an epidural when I wanted it. I want to see the sister."

There must be something in my tone that warns her not to argue because she meekly follows orders. In comes the sister. She hoists my legs up and examines me and I feel I am in good hands. The next thing she drops my legs, turns and runs to the door. "The baby is coming, I must call the doctor!"

Suddenly I realise what is happening. I have never gone to special classes for giving birth nor learnt any special breathing exercises. In fact, I have very little idea of the birth process. As each pain comes, I expect the next to be more excruciating and the final push as the baby emerges to be the most painful. This is what they show in the movies and that is where my knowledge starts and ends. The first two months after this child was conceived, we were in hiding from the police. For the next two months we were in detention. Police were conducting door to door searches in Athlone and Wynberg. They were entering mosques and beating schoolchildren and their parents. There wasn't time to think about what was happening to my body. I was just trying to stay alive. The few times I went to see the gynaecologist, he was more interested in me providing him with explanations of arms caches in Guguletu, than he was in providing me with details of my condition. However, his attitude did convey to me that all was well and that I was strong and doing just fine.

Now my body dominates my world. It takes over, no longer allowing me to ignore it. As the pain shoots through my back, I think only of the next wave, grateful that I can endure this one.

Then pressure pulsates through my body so strongly that I realise I cannot stop it. I feel instinctively that I must push. "Help me, nurse," I call to her. "The baby is coming."

"The baby cannot come now," she says striding confidently to the foot of the bed.

"The doctor is not here."

She takes hold of both my ankles and crosses my legs. "Don't push now, mummy, you will hurt the baby's head. You must wait, the doctor is not here yet."

Oh dear God. I don't want to hurt my baby's head. I am trying my best not to push. So I pull onto the steel frame of the bed and draw in my breath in an attempt to prevent the baby from coming. With my legs crossed, there is little I can do but gasp and try and hold it in. It's a pretty impossible task. Giving birth has it's own time. Most of us know that feeling of desperation when we rush to find a public toilet. When it wants to come out, it wants to come out.

Sweat is pouring from my forehead. I can feel the red-hot flush on my face. I will myself to keep calm and happy as I bring this child into the world. I must forget that I am lying here all alone because those same men who had defiled me are now hunting my husband. I must suppress the need to touch his curly black hair that softens his tense dark face.

I have no way of knowing what has happened or why he has not come. And this is not the time to think about it.

The door opens and it's Dr Samie, clad in a white coat with a stethoscope dangling around his neck. There is no time to explain what the nurse has been doing. He quickly helps to place my legs in the stirrups. He talks with me gently: "You have done well, you have done well. Push, Zubeida, push. I can see the head."

I push and push and with ease, I bring my daughter into this world. There is no pain as she slides out of me like a fish slithering through water.

"It's a girl! A girl!"

Her firm body lies wet against my stomach where the sister places her. I am immediately aware of her body. Firm and not floppy. Her arms are strong. Her legs are strong and her tiny fingers are long and beautiful. I uncurl her fingers and place my little finger in her right hand. She clamps it tight and like a jolt of electricity, I feel her strength bolting through my finger, up my arm and into my heart.

This is the little baby the lieutenant had threatened to kill, to burn out of my body. This is part of my flesh and blood that could have brought about my spiritual death.

She has slipped out so easily – I had expected that final effort to be agonising – here she is born at 6:40 a.m. on 27 June 1986 in defiance of all that we have both endured. The nurse lifts her onto a white towel, wraps her up and carries her away for her first wash.

My long black hair lies wet on the hospital pillow, as if I have just come out of the rain. The light of the morning is slowly filtering through the high barred window at the far end of the ward. My mind is a blank as I drop off to sleep, empty of all the uncertainties.

CHAPTER TWO

I am sipping a cup of hot tea. The baby is in the nursery and I have been tidied up, dressed in a freshly-starched white St Monica's nightie with my hair brushed back. I am feeling sleepy but happy. My eyes are heavy.

I ask no questions. I place the cup on the side table and doze off again. Then I hear familiar voices. I open my eyes and see my mom and dad. My chest constricts. My eyes are stinging. The tears flow silently down my mom's cheeks as she holds me. It's hard not to cry. Suddenly I visualise her on her back in our Claremont home. A small cottage on Lansdowne Road in an area soon to be declared white. For the first time I understand the enormity of her life. She had given birth to me with a midwife by her side, her husband and children hovering at the door and her sister, Rashieda, close at hand. I was her fifth child and second daughter. I understand for the first time what that meant, that she had endured this six times over.

We hug, crying. My dad is praying. "Where is the baby?" he asks.

"In the nursery." He swings away from the bed and goes through the door and down the corridor. He is not one to sit still much.

The next minute he is back. "They won't let me see the baby," he says.

"Why?" says my mom.

"It's against the rules," he says. "Only the father can see the baby."

"Against the rules?" says my mom. "Against the rules? This is my grandchild. They cannot stop me from seeing my grandchild."

Oh glory be. What am I going to do now? I can see they are upset. Especially my mother. I have never seen her so irate. I decide not to get involved. It is too much to have a drama now I think. But a drama there will be. My dad assures my mom that he will sort it out. He has a persuasive way with people so he is confident. He wanders off again to find the sister on duty.

It is not the first time that my mother has been deprived of enjoying the birth of a grandchild. And it is not the first time that I have this strong feeling of culpability for her distress. Six years ago, on 7 September, 1980, I saw my parents in a small room at security headquarters in Port Elizabeth. On that same day, my sister Julie gave birth to her baby son, Junaid. My big sister, large limpid eyes in a light-brown face, an Eastern Cape Aloe, delicate-looking on the outside yet strong on the inside.

I say very little. What is there to say at a time like this? It is bittersweet. I am happy yet sad. I am nervous that at any minute the police will arrive. What if they know I am here and barge in to question me about my husband? Will I be able to bear it? Let me not think of this.

"What lovely flowers, mom. Thanks."

"We also brought you chocolates, darling. You must just rest. Why did you not call me to be here with you last night?" she says.

"I was afraid that the police would follow you and I wanted Johnny to be here with me, but there seems to have been some confusion," I say.

"Anyway, we are here now. But I don't think it's safe for you to come home with us," she says. "Where will you go?"

"I don't know."

"Don't worry we will make a plan. We will find a place where you will not be harassed," she says. My dear mom. Always the practical one.

Dad is heading back to us with a jaunty stride. He cuts a colourful figure with his dark-red fez on which hangs a black tassle similar to those attached to university graduation caps. He is one of the last of his generation to maintain the Moroccan headgear made popular by Muslims at the Cape in the last century. He has persuaded the sister to let him see Ruschka.

"I told her that I have to pray in her ear," he says.

"So she let you see her?" says my mom.

"Yes."

Into her ear he had whispered the sweet Arabic words that accompany the daily life of every Muslim. "I believe that there is no God but God and that Muhammad is the messenger of God." He then recited the athān (the daily call to prayer) that floats out five times a day from mosque turrets all over the world. "God is Great (x4). I declare that there is no God but God (x2). I declare that Muhammad (Peace be upon him) is His messenger (x2). Come to prayer (x2) Come to success (x2) God is Great (x2). There is no God but God."

I can see that he is happy to have done his duty, but my mother is furious. She too wants to see her grandchild. The sister comes and my dad thanks her and asks if my mom can also see Ruschka. She says no. Then my dad commits the ultimate sin. He takes the box of chocolates that mom has brought for me and hands it to the sister in appreciation. It is so typically my father. My mother is ready to have a fit.

"You come home today!" she says to me. 'This is ridiculous! Imagine! I can't see my own grandchild! Never heard of such rules."

But I am not eager to go home because there is no home to go to really. We have rented a house in Parkwood, about five kilometres from my family home in Wynberg, but it is hard to call it a home because we had moved there barely three months previously after both being released from detention and before the three months were up I had fled. Memories come pouring back again as I wait in my hospital bed next to my irate mother.

I remember that sunny afternoon when Mostert arrived, forcing me to abandon the house.

I am alone. Johnny is in hiding. He always has this uncanny sense of how the mood is changing in the country. It was that sixth sense and his amazing organisational ability that attracted me to him. Days before the state of emergency was declared, he warned that they would come for him. And they did but he was not home. He had been in hiding two weeks before the arrests started. I stayed on in the hope that everything would settle soon and we would go back to normal. We had prepared the cot and tidied the house in preparation for the visitors we knew would come to see the baby. A new lounge suite. A chest of drawers to pack her tiny little garments into.

There is a knock on the door and I see a hand coming through the window next to it, moving aside the curtain. I am expecting my dad to fetch me so I am not on my guard. But the arm is a pink arm and then I see his face. It is Mostert. I draw back in horror. "Maak oop, Zubeida. Maak oop." (Open up, Zubeida. Open up.)

There is no telephone in the house, so I cannot call for help. I am not keen to let him into the house because I cannot stand the thought of him being near me. Especially when I am days away from giving birth. I am like a young lioness protecting her cub, moving from one room to the other, uncertain what to do. Trapped. I just do not want him up close to me or my baby – to smell his sour odour, evoking in me the memory of helpless isolation. He walks around the house, banging on the back door. Banging on the windows. Then around the front again. I do not open. I watch until I see him walking to the street and I can no longer see him. Perhaps he is in his car. The car is still there.

I quickly open the door and lock it behind me, walking straight to the gate and out into the street. I walk right past the car with my huge belly swaying from side to side. He jumps out of the car when he sees me and runs after me but I ignore him and keep on walking, straight to a neighbour who lets me call my brother Sulaiman. We arrange that he will ask the local shopkeeper to open his back gate so that he can pull his car into the back yard. I leave the bewildered neighbour and cross the street to the shop with Mostert following in his car. Fortunately he does not run into the shop, choosing instead to wait in his car. With the permission of the shopkeeper, I walk through the storeroom and out of the back door where I wait for five minutes before my brother arrives and whisks me away to safety.

Since that day, two weeks ago, I have not been back to the house.

"We will work it out," says my mom. "Don't worry."

They leave me to sleep again.

The next day, Johnny takes the risk of coming to see us. He had sent flowers earlier and a sweet note of love. When I see him, tall and strong next to my bed, we are both quietly happy. No questions are asked. I know it's too much to try and understand why he did not arrive at the hospital two nights earlier. I slip my small hand into his, slender and strong. Our fingers intertwine, cutting off any desire to face uncomfortable detail. It is enough that he is here now. The feeling of his rough tweed jacket against my cheek reassures me. The muscled arms around my body satisfy the need for solace. They allow him to visit the nursery and he thanks me for giving him another daughter. He has a daughter, Leila, by his first marriage, and two sons, Yasser and Fidel.

I am used to this life of not expecting too much. Of not knowing from one minute to the next who is alive and who is dead. Of whether I will see him again. So each moment is precious. Each moment is valued and intense. He stays for a few minutes and then is gone. But I know how to reach him, so I am happy.

I stretch my stay until Sunday morning. I am not keen to leave the hospital. Here I feel a bit safe and assured of some solitude. But my mother is now beside herself. I have to leave the hospital so that she can see her granddaughter.

They arrive with warm clothes for us. We are both bundled up against the cold before being led to the waiting car. My mother holds Ruschka firmly in her arms, reluctant to let go.

They have decided to take me to my brother's home in Grassy Park. "I think that is best," says my mom. "The cops have never been to his house and they don't know him," she says. "You can be comfortable there."

19

I don't argue. I am just grateful they have sorted it all out for me.

In Grassy Park, my sister-in-law, Razia, has kindly moved her son, Khalil, out of his room so that I can have a room to myself. And so I embark on the unpredictable road of motherhood.

The pump clamps tight against my breast which I am holding over the bathroom basin. I struggle to stimulate the flow of milk that will nourish my child. Motherhood is a more complicated matter than I expected – breastfeeding is not coming naturally to me. And as the raw red nipples become more painful with each feed, the tension in me grows, gripping my body like the tentacles of an octopus. The hard work is just beginning. It's funny how often the emphasis is on the trials and tribulations of the pregnancy and the birth process and not on what comes afterwards. In a few short hours, it is beginning to dawn on me that perhaps I am in for a rougher ride than I expected.

There had been so many visitors the night before, some to see me and others to greet my brother and his wife, who were leaving on a pilgrimage to Mecca. The sweetest visitor was trade unionist Zora Mehlomakhulu who, with Virginia Engel and Oscar Mphetha, had taught me all I know about organizing workers. She had other skills too, it turned out. She brought a gift for the baby. Wrapped in soft tissue paper, a pair of baby's booties, a matinee jacket, a cap and a shawl, which she had hand-knitted in apple-green wool and ribbons so they would suit a boy or a girl. In her busy schedule she had taken the time to make a gift for my child with her own hands. Beautiful, majestic Zora. If you had to see her on the Mowbray bus travelling to her home in Langa in the late afternoon, you would not look twice. She could just be another domestic worker, with her scarf tied tightly around her head and her carrier bag on the seat beside her. But she was the one who for years had quietly rebuilt the trade union movement after it was crushed at the end of the fifties.

When I give up on the breast pump and return to my room I touch Zora's delicate hand-work and then sit quietly on the single bed, watching my baby in the carrycot next to me. Her mop of hair is as black as ever but her rumpled face is slowly losing its creases. We are both at peace. I savour the quiet, enjoying the faint winter sun peeping through the drawn curtains. Perhaps I can try to read a bit. Perhaps I should rather sleep. They say it's good to sleep when the baby sleeps. To take the gap. I rest my back against the pillow, relieved that we are safe and happy. I close my eyes. But then I hear the doorbell ringing.

My father had arrived earlier and he goes to the door. I hear a noise. Loud voices. I sit up. My father is coming down the passage with somebody. I really don't feel like a visitor now but anyway that is the way of the community. Neighbours, friends, relatives descend upon one when a child is born.

I remember when I was released from detention in 1980, I had the same experience of communal outpouring of care. Then I was barely given time to get out of my pyjamas in the morning before the visitors started arriving. It is just the custom.

I straighten the bedspread and lower my legs to the floor. The door creaks open, swinging inwards into the tiny room. Then I see him. Pink, red face, light-brown hair, liquor-bloated body in a cream safari suit. This man who had tried to burn my baby from my body. He steps into the room in the direction of my child, his signature odour wafting towards me. I am screaming, shouting – but not moving.

"Get out! Get out! Dad, take him out of here. Don't let him look at Ruschka!"

I turn my head from side to side looking for an object I can fling at him to protect myself.

He steps back, grinning, as my father tries to persuade him to leave me alone. The hysteria surges up in me, taking over, snatching control of my body. I cannot think. The emotions are too strong. I follow him and my dad to the front door, shouting like a woman possessed until he leaves. Nothing can make me stay now. I have to find a place where I can be at peace with my baby. I have to.

CHAPTER THREE

I lay Ruschka down in the centre of the bed even though she is too young to roll off. She is dressed in white flannel leggings and a pink knitted matinée jacket. I use the throw-away diapers sparingly because they are so expensive and I have my batch of cloth diapers with large safety pins stacked in a colourful bag. I am so relieved that she has dropped off to sleep because I would like to be in the gathering when the proceedings start. I am in my brother's bedroom and he and his wife are at the front of the house, hugging their tearful children. The time has come to say goodbye. This morning they leave on their long journey for Mecca and the house is filled with relatives, friends and neighbours.

I arrived early this morning so that I could settle Ruschka and be with them. I try to block out the memory of last week's drama, which had forced me to leave the comfort of my nephew's room, to take my three-day-old child and move yet again.

A friend, Shireen Misbach, and her family took us in. She was one of those who provided one of the many safe houses for activists during those years. With five children of her own, Shireen eased me into the routine of bathing my baby, folding her diaper so that the pins would not hurt and watching for any signs of yellow jaundice, common in young babies, she told me. Plucked away from my family, again in a different environment, I felt dazed most of the time.

Shireen, her sleek brown hair swept into a bun in the nape of her neck, found a friend to bring me to my brother's home this morning. From here I will go back to my mother's home in Wynberg. I cannot keep on moving. Not with Ruschka around, and it would not be wise to stay on my own in the Parkwood house.

Razia and Sulaiman have said their special departure prayers in the privacy of their room but now they are dressed and ready for the communal farewell. My brother is dressed in a three-piece grey suit, a white shirt and has a white starched cap perched on his head. My sister-in-law, whom I prefer to call my sister, has a plain cream headscarf falling across her shoulders to down below her elbows. The scarf is draped around a soft reddish floral dress that reaches her ankles. On her chest is pinned a white orchid

22

arranged against a fine fern sprig sent with well wishes from my sister Julie, who is in London.

They stand together in the entrance hall of their home, waiting for the arrival of the priest who is to perform the farewell ceremony.

I hear a booming voice greeting the congregants at the door and I know he has arrived. I cannot see him but I know Sheikh Nazeem Mohammed is towering above everybody else with his distinctive white Arab scarf on his head and his long flowing robe, either black or white. He is an unusually tall man. His mother was a big woman. For as long as I can remember he has been in my life. As a child I used to accompany my dad to a particular building site in Bega Road, Wynberg, on many a Sunday morning. Sheikh Nazeem was there with other locals, some of us carrying bricks to others who built them into walls. It took a good year or two to complete because it depended on voluntary work, but in the end we had our madressa, an Islamic learning centre and a hall for community activities. It was called the Vigilance Hall and was run by the Vigilance Association, of which my dad was an executive member.

Sheikh Nazeem had a special relationship with my dad, a complex one over the years but a special one. He officiated at all family functions and had sanctified my marriage vows. When faced with the threats of torture in detention, I had sent him a letter written on toilet paper that I had smuggled out of my cell and he had not failed to act.

There is a certain strength in his booming voice, it calms me as the sea does when it thuds against dark-brown boulders on our coastline. I can hear my dad fussing and offering him tea. On the table, the family has arranged an array of tasty offerings for the early-morning visitors – koesisters, pies, corned-meat sandwiches and other delicacies offered on Cape Muslim tables.

Koesisters, a special favourite eaten every Sunday morning in most homes, are doughnuts, spiced with cardamon, cinamon, fine dried citrus peel, dunked in syrup and sprinkled with coconut. They are part of a delightful food regimen that sticks this community together like toffy.

Sheikh, as we all refer to him, calls my dad.

"Hassan, ons gaan nou begin." (Hassan, we are going to start now.) He raises both hands, cupping them slightly, holding them in line with his chest. We all rise and soon the chanting begins, bringing a sense of peace.

Our ancestors who developed these rituals possessed true wisdom. The melodious arabic chanting has a way of binding everybody together. We all say the same words, over and over again and it somehow calms the mind and strengthens the spirit. I wonder if Ruschka can hear it all through her sleep.

I cannot stand for long because I still feel a bit weak after the birth. I pull a chair into the passage and sit down. Next to me is my sister-in-law Zerene and next to her is my Aunty Janap. Both women have husbands in detention. So the three of us are bound together through common experience.

My third-eldest brother, Adam, who is Zerene's husband, had been detained three weeks ago on 14 June 1986, just when the second state of emergency was declared. He was going about his normal butcher duties that Saturday morning, when a policeman walked into his shop and tore off a poster on the window. My youngest brother, Mansoor, had asked him to display the poster calling for a work stayaway on 16 June 1986 to commemorate the tenth anniversary of the Soweto uprisings and massacre. He had obliged, as had many other business people in Wynberg.

At the same time as one group entered the butchery, another group of policemen arrived at the premises of Adam's other business in Broad Road, Wynberg. He had just taken over the petrol station and was in the process of giving up the butchery. There was excitement when the policemen found a stack of pamphlets on the counter of the petrol station shop. With his manager, Faried Akleker, they searched the premises and found further batches of the "Eid" pamphlet. They radioed for help and ordered Faried to ask Adam to come to the premises.

Leaving the busy butchery on a Saturday morning, he arrived at the petrol station to find small batches of pamphlets stacked in the reception area. He was then told to go to the Wynberg Police Station to answer a few questions. Instead of being questioned, he found himself whisked away to Victor Verster prison, dressed in his bloodied white butcher's coat.

He has been detained there in terms of the emergency laws ever since. So now my sister-in-law and I sit alone in the passage.

At Victor Verster, they were seven on that first day that my brother was arrested, then the next day, police arrested the entire St Nicholas Church Congregation in Elsies River and they joined them. Men and women in their Sunday best, suits and church hats tried to make themselves comfortable on the cold cement floors with hard felt mats for beds.

On the third day, Adam was standing in line for his daily food ration when he saw his uncle. My uncle Khalid, my mother's youngest brother, was principal of Alexander Sinton High School in Athlone – one of the schools at the hub of student uprisings in the Peninsula.

The school was one of the few in the black community that had a hall and this gave it a special attraction for the many young people trying to organise resistance. Meetings at other schools had to take place in exposed open areas, making them easy targets for police attack. So they drifted to Alexander Sinton.

I remember the drama last year when parents, teachers and children throughout the Cape decided to defy the local education minister, Carter Ebrahim. Mr Ebrahim, who had been dredged up from the ranks of unemployed teachers to become minister for the "coloured" schools, had decided to close schools for three days to bring an end to protests.

Parents, teachers and pupils at high schools decided in return to defy the closure and open their schools. Primary schools followed suit. My uncle unlocked the school gate, allowing parents and children to pour into the school that morning. Three cops arrived, placing everybody under arrest. But they soon discovered they had a problem. They were under siege because other parents, who arrived later, realised what was going on and managed to block the school entrance. They pulled their cars in front of the school gate to prevent police reinforcements from coming through. Slowly a winding snake of cars piled up all along Thornton Road, making vehicle entry into the school impossible. The three men radioed for help. But by then, some pupils had stopped a bus driver and asked him to move his bus across the road. He was very happy to oblige. Once parked, he removed his key from the ignition, got down onto the road and walked away.

With teargas, a helicopter and truckloads of reinforcements, the police finally made their way into the school and arrested everybody. My uncle Khalid was the final one herded into the last of four trucks that bolted at breakneck speed down Thornton Road to the Manenberg Police Station, ignoring all stop streets and red traffic lights. In the vicinity of the school, hordes of onlookers found themselves being chased by quirt-wielding riot police, shooting tear-gas. A quirt is a long thin rubber rod that burned dark red weals into human flesh. On that day, I was trying to hide behind a flower pot in somebody's garden but a quirt found me.

My aunt is the boisterous, chatty type but this morning, she is subdued. They have removed my uncle from Victor Verster prison and taken him to the intensive care unit at City Park Hospital where he is being treated for a collapsed lung and a heart condition. She is very worried, as are we all.

Sheikh is coming to the end of the Arabic prayers. A certain ease has descended upon everybody and then Sheikh begins to speak: "This is not a normal time in our country," he says. "It is in very difficult times that Sulaiman and Razia make this journey. They have to leave behind their parents, who are struggling to cope with a son who is in detention and another son, Mansoor, who is on the run. Raghmie, the mother of this family, also has a brother in detention. Khalid Desai is one of our teachers and a principal and is locked up even though he is very sick. And Zubeida is here with her little baby recovering from her detention. This has been going on for a long time . . ."

As he speaks, I feel a pain in my heart that moves to my throat, choking me. Yes, this has been going on for six years now. After my detention and torture as a reporter at the *Cape Times*, the security police became a constant feature in my life. They were there when I got off the train in the mornings on my way to work. They were there to slap a further subpoena on me as I stepped down from the dock after being acquitted for the possession of three banned books. They withdrew my passport the day after I reported that students at the University of the Western Cape had burnt an apartheid flag and raised an ANC flag. It was endless.

I lower my head in an attempt to conceal the tears that threaten to spill over my lids but then they come flooding out in an unstoppable torrent. It's hard for me to think about the periods of torture and detention. The tears that come now I attribute to post-natal depression. As soon as I start crying, Zerene next to me begins to sob as well, then my aunty Jane next to her and then the three of us set everybody off in a chain reaction.

We have never known this kind of sorrow as children. My dad would say: "Laugh!" Then one of the six would try to force the gustiest of laughs, which would set off a more natural guffaw from the next and then on to the next. As my sister Julie would always say, we had difficulties but no sorrows. Our parents spared us the best they could. History did not allow us to accord them the same privilege.

I cry for my child, my husband, my family and my comrades. Zerene cries for her Adam, having no idea why she is in the situation she is in. Aunty Jane is crying for her Khalid, whom she fears may be dying. A few days earlier she had lived through a rumour that he had in fact died. Through the house and outside on the stoep, men and women, young and old, shoulders touching, cry for their own personal anguish and ours.

A week later, Zerene calls me to say that the lawyer is unsure whether it is possible to bring an interdict for Adam's release. I leave Ruschka with my mom and accompany Zerene to Abdurauf Pohplonker's office in Retreat Road. He runs both a legal practice and a family butchery inherited from his father. The Pohplonkers are bound to Retreat as the Sisulus are to Soweto, their lives intimately intertwined with the local community. Many a Saturday morning we erected a makeshift table in front of their shop to hold a rummage sale. The crowds meandering along the road very quickly bought up our goods. It was an easy way to raise money for the youth and civic organisations in neighbouring Lavender Hill. While some of us sold clothes, other volunteers distributed the community newspaper *Grassroots* to passers-by. Through the newspaper, we initiated community organisations that in combination sprouted into the powerful United Democratic Front, spearheading the movement against apartheid.

It is the first time that I see Abdurauf in his legal practice. It is a rather different Rauf to the one I usually see behind the meat counter at Poppy's Meat Market. He is casually dressed in a shirt, pants and pullover jersey.

I sense that he is nervous. Adam is not only a client but also a good friend and the chairman of the Chamber of Muslim Meat Traders (COMMTRA), of which he is a member. He wants to give this case his best shot but the justice system has become one of the first casualties of the state of emergency. He is unsure whether he can successfully interdict the state. Zerene says very little. All she wants is for her husband to come home.

"We can only do it and see what happens," I say to him. "If he is not released, then at least we have put his case on record."

The lawyers are always looking at the matter only from a legal point of view. We are always trying to push the boundaries of the law to make a political statement.

He agrees to collect sworn statements from all relevant parties and to give notice of our intention to interdict the court to release Adam.

A few days later we are back in his office. We study the sworn statement of Faried Akleker, the manager of Adam's petrol station. He swears that the police had at no stage told Adam that the poster and Eid pamphlet were illegal. Eid is the Muslim holiday which follows at the end of Ramadān. In her statement, however, my mother says that the police insisted the posters and pamphlets were subversive.

"I told the policeman that there was nothing subversive about the poster and that similar posters were displayed at various shops all over Wynberg.

I also told them that the pamphlets were handed out at mosques on Eid day and were quite harmless."

With all due respect to my mom, calling on people to stay away from work could indeed be considered subversive. By then the range of "subversive activities" had become so broad that it was natural for us to view any such suggestion as suspect. It was subversive to read banned books freely available abroad. It was subversive to write about police brutality. It was subversive to hang a poster in a tree in front of your house calling for the release of your son.

In September 1985 my mom had attached a placard to a broomstick and suspended it from a tree in her front garden to make people aware that my youngest brother, Mansoor, was in detention. "Release my son and all other detainees." Armed men in casspirs had moved into Wynberg and ripped the placard from the tree.

We go to court ten days later. The matter is set down for 10 a.m. on 24 July 1986. Warrant Officer Jacobus Stipp, a tall white policeman, tells the court that the posters incited people to stay away from work. He also tells the court that the posters were pasted inside the window of the butchery and not on the outside as was the case at other businesses. "It would have been a difficult task to confront shopowners with this, since they could easily argue that it was the work of passers-by," says Stipp.

He denies that he had made the manager, Faried Akleker, call my brother to come to the petrol station without admitting that the police were requesting his presence. He also explains why he informed Adam that he was being detained only once he was at the police station.

"I first went through the stack of pamphlets which we had confiscated during the investigation," he says. "I could not find anything related to June 16 but I came to the conclusion that the accused identified with the objectives of the stayaway call made on the poster and decided that it was in the interests of public order and ending the state of emergency to arrest and detain him."

At the end of the day, the court adjourns. Judgement is to be given first thing the next morning.

"All rise in court," says the clerk as the Honourable Mr Justice Berman sweeps in.

I can see Zerene's face becoming hotter and hotter as he drones on, summarising every detail of Adam's arrest. We are not interested in the detail. We just want him to come to the conclusion. Adam has been in detention for six weeks already and for Zerene and her four-year-old son, it is becoming unbearable.

"Having heard Counsel for the applicant and having read the documents filed of record," says Justice Berman, "I order that the continued detention of Adam Jaffer be declared unlawful. And that the said Adam Jaffer be released forthwith from the Victor Verster Prison."

I hug Zerene and my dad. We hold hands, the three of us, as we wait for the words to end so that we can rush to fetch my brother.

"I further award costs against the Minister of Justice and the Minister of Law and Order. This court is adjourned for the day."

"All rise," says the clerk, and Justice Berman exits.

I run to thank Rauf and as I shake his hand the relief is visible on his face. He is clearing away the documents spread across the court bench as we wait for the final release papers. On top of the pile of documents is Annexure A: the "subversive" Eid pamphlet that prompted the police to call in reinforcements at my brother's petrol station.

I sit down to read the full text for the first time.

It starts with a quote from the Holy Qur'ān discouraging lavishness.

And act not wastefully (i.e unproductively). Lo! He approveth not the wasters. (VI: 141)

The text explains that Muslims are urged to help families in need. To spare a thought for the families of those in detention, on the run, for those schoolchildren who have been sjambokked.

"The circumstances of many Muslim families in the Cape are critical. Let us cut down on our lavish spending on clothes and food. Let us divert some of this money to organisations that are providing food to needy Muslim families on Eid day," the text reads.

The Holy Qur'ān does not permit men to speak harshly to their female partners, the text goes on, to abuse them, to take drugs and alcohol and neglect their children. Yet these are widespread growing phenomena that require frank discussion.

I find myself reflecting on how often the basic guidelines of the religion play second fiddle to an obsession with controlling women. Instead of examining the needs of the most needy, men are reminded to keep their wives in check – the wives must cover their heads and be good Muslim women.

29

But it is not the women who are the greatest threat to the disintegration of this community. Many a time, they fend for the children on their own and invest time and energy in religious ritual that fosters continuity from generation to generation.

If only the authority of the Holy Qur'ān as evoked in the conclusion of the pamphlet could be commonplace.

. . . and squander not (thy wealth) in wantonness. Lo! the squanderers were ever companions of the devil, and the devil was ever an ingrate to his Lord." (XVII: 26-27)

Carefully typed in small print at the bottom of the pamphlet is a list of local organisations endorsing the call: The Chamber of Muslim Meat Traders (COMMTRA), the Muslim Judicial Council (MJC), the Muslim Youth Movement (MYM), the Cape Vigilance Association, the Muslim Students Association, the Islamic Medical Association and the Call of Islam.

I hand the pamphlet back to Rauf as he stacks the last papers into his briefcase. Despite the court victory today, I cannot help thinking that Adam's case is a sharp reminder that the definition of "subversive activities" is fast losing all boundaries.

CHAPTER FOUR

M y head pounds, my heart pounds, my innards are coming out. I think
and see nothing else. My legs are running, moving my body forward,
a body still heavy with the weight I had gained during my pregnancy. I
will have to diet. The birth of my baby, now nine weeks old, has only re-
duced my weight by a few kilograms.

I run right into Mostert, grabbing at the lapels of his jacket and holding
on as tight as I can, screaming all the while. My whole personality is changing. I am screaming more and more. As I do, I understand Winnie Mandela
better. The strongest piece of iron will bend when sufficient heat is applied.
I have one objective and one objective only – to prevent Mostert from shooting my husband, from taking away from me the man who is the father of
my child and whom I love very deeply.

I hold on tight, demanding to know what he is doing here and what right
he has to come and interfere with us. I am bordering on the hysterical: "He
just came to see his daughter. He just came to see his daughter. I will not
let you take him away."

There is no need for me to hold on to his lapels quite so tightly. He could
get away in any case if he wants to. He is a big burly man and I have small
hands. Instead, he stands rooted to the spot, completely disarmed, unable
to move. I let go when I realise that he cannot move, he is not moving. He
does not know what to do and Johnny is getting enough time to get away.

S.T.O.P. STOP. It is like the game we used to play as children. My friends
run. I spell out the word, shout STOP and they stop and freeze. When I start
spelling again, they come alive and rush forward.

As Johnny flees, my brother Mansoor, who is also in hiding, quietly slips
out of the front door and seeks refuge in the squash court nearby.

Then a uniformed policeman makes his appearance at the side of the
house, with more policemen following. The lieutenant comes alive again
and rushes forward.

With a cocked gun, he runs into my mother's house, trying his best to
regain his composure. WAA, WAA, WAA . . . Oops, my mother is doing it
again. She sets off the burglar alarm. Pandemonium breaks loose. Cops run
in all directions. "Daar trip hy die alarm!" (He's tripped the alarm), shouts

the lieutenant and runs into the room where he expects to find my husband. My mother is holding Ruschka. I take her into my arms.

Setting off the burglar alarm has become my mother's only protection against these men when they invade her privacy. When they come at night, the alarm alerts the neighbours and they come trooping into the house, with nightgowns tightly covering their nervousness. They come to witness the actions of men who seek the obscurity of the night to hide their aggression.

Now in the midday heat they gather on the pavements outside watching another carload of police arrive and come dashing into our house. The high school close by has just been dismissed and pupils are pouring through the gates, pausing on both sides of the road to watch the unfolding drama.

I have my daughter cradled in one arm and am standing in the dining room where I can see both the front door and the entrance to the room into which Mostert has run. "Wat is dit, wat is dit?" (What is it, what is it?) say the new batch of cops who are just arriving. "Is dit huisbraak?" (Is it a burglary?)

In the end there are cops all over. In the lanes on both sides of the house where I used to play as a child, in all the rooms, looking under beds, opening cupboards. We should be used to this by now. It has happened so many times. Yet each time, the shock is different.

They search for him across the lanes, in the houses next door, on the right-hand side of ours, searching without luck. He is hidden away by a high school girl in a house to the left, in the next road. They follow the trail on the right through an open window where he dropped the sandwich he was eating.

The lieutenant turns his attention to me. "Vat haar weg!" (Take her away) he orders one of his men, who drags me off the pavement and across the street to where a police van is waiting. I feel like one of the drunks they toss into the vans on a Friday night when they come speeding down our back street. He pushes me into the back of the van with no regard for the baby in my arms.

Beads of sweat gather on her tiny brow. She is so unusually quiet. With one arm, I hold her tightly against my breast. With the other, I try to find a grip on the roof of the police van. They are driving at a tremendous speed. I concentrate all my efforts on ensuring that I am not flung across the van, hurting my child. I am stiff as a board as they swing around the corners, making their way to Wynberg Police station. And all the while her round eyes look up at me. She is so unusually quiet. I expect her to wail. But she is quiet. As if she understands.

For a moment I wonder if she will one day regret this life into which she has been born. No frills and soft cots for her. Just motion. Constant motion. From one place to another. For the past five years, the pressure has been relentless. Detentions, arrests, beatings, shootings, teargas. But then I was on my own. Now I have her. A child, nine weeks old, with a tough body but a soft heart who is sending me a message: Handle with care.

CHAPTER FIVE

I take my seat in the public gallery. Ruschka is at home with my mom, freeing me to concentrate on this trial. I am worried. What if Elizabeth and Fuad go to jail? I will feel so responsible. They are being charged for making flags that I had asked them to make.

Elizabeth Erasmus is accused number one. Next to her in the dock stands Fuad Carlie, an immaculate businessman, nattily dressed in suit and tie. Elizabeth is wearing the khaki volunteer uniform of the ANC with black, green and gold beads threaded onto numerous braids hanging down to her shoulders. Advocate Siraj Desai had a fit at the start of this trial when Elizabeth arrived at court.

"How am I supposed to defend her when she comes here dressed like that?" he asked me.

"She wants to make a point," I said.

"It's exactly a point I don't want her to make," he said, shaking his head.

It is hard to imagine two accused more different. I met Elizabeth when one of her co-workers at Cape Underwear called us saying that they wanted to join the union. Last year, she had left the factory and become my assistant. Fuad Carlie is a neighbour and owns a clothing wholesale company. He had persuaded his former business partner to allow him to use his factory at night.

Caught red-handed sewing reams of black, green and gold cloths, the two stand accused of furthering the aims of the ANC.

When the case was first brought to him, Desai was confident he could win it on straight legal grounds. But with time, he was beginning to think otherwise.

"Zubeida, the top brass of the security police are all around the prosecutor. They are treating this case as a priority. I must warn you that the stakes are high."

As I sit listening to the magistrate summing up the trial, it is clear that the court faces a dilemma. The state has presented no facts to explain to the court why the flags were being made, if indeed the cloths were flags.

This business about facts that condemn people hurtles me back to the past, back to that moment when Mostert left the cell after threatening to burn my baby from my womb. I thank God for the strength given to me during those many hours. If my strength had failed me as it had done in 1980, the state would have had its facts.

I relive those crucial hours. I am back in the cell. Back and forth. Back and forth I rock gently on the bed in indecision. I wish the policewoman would move away from the door so that I could write. They do not know I have a pen. My mom had hidden it in the crevice of my suitcase and by chance I had discovered it after many days in detention. I could write onto the toilet paper to try and resolve my dilemma. I always find it much easier to write down my problems. It helps me think.

Back and forth, the options bounce about in my head. I sift through all the possibilities. For the first time, I seriously consider what would happen if I were to give him the information he wants. I am experienced enough to understand that he needs it to make a case against us.

Without the information in my possession, he has a very weak case. Two of the elderly women arrested are members of the Clothing Workers Union of which I am general secretary. It's not hard to imagine how anxious their families must be. The other women are activists, so it bothers me less. The man arrested is a neighbour. I feel so responsible for their plight.

There is a chance that they will all be released if I cooperate. Part of me wants to cooperate so that they can be set free. But most of all I want to cooperate for my baby's sake. I want her so much. If I tell them what they want to know and we all go on trial, then we could be released on bail before facing a jail sentence. But what if I get off and the others are sent to jail? How would I face Ruschka one day and tell her that in order to give her life, I betrayed my comrades? Some kind person would love to tell her even if I did not and then she would suffer.

I just cannot do this to her. But then perhaps I have to do it for her. Surely my comrades would understand. What if I lost her? She is a small, helpless growing fetus, a fusion of my love for my husband and his for me, with a right to come into this world.

But then would that fetus not be able to withstand this chemical the lieutenant is preparing for me?

When he steps through the door on this January afternoon, cooled only by the breeze blowing off Sea Point beach, with my face glowing I block out the sound of the traffic and the lone bird singing outside and brace myself.

I have tied my hair back with a scarf and am wearing the white and black floral maternity dress my mom sent me.

He paces up and down the cell, opening my small suitcase and lifting up each article of clothing. He is considering taking all these away so that I will not be so comfortable, he says. He is so relaxed, certain that he has me under his control.

He speaks as if he is the father and I the child.

"Come now, Zubeida, as soon as you answer my questions, I will personally take you home.

"If you don't, you will lose your baby and never see your husband again. He is going to hang himself in his cell with his pillowcases soon. We are making the preparations. He is already taking those small pills."

He grins and I smell the sour smell steaming through his pores.

"Now tell me, why were you making those flags? Why?"

I have rehearsed this moment many times. Please Allah, give me the strength to do it: "You can do what you want to do. I cannot stop you but don't expect me to cooperate with you. I see no reason to answer your questions. Do whatever you feel you must do. You stand for apartheid. I am against it. I have nothing to say to you."

For a moment he cannot speak. His instincts are probably prompting him to slap me or to stand on me as he had on activist June Esau, but he has to be mindful of the publicity around my case. He had been so sure of himself, so sure that he had made a break-through and now this. He swings towards the door and leaves, mumbling something about leaving me to rot in the cell.

If I could have opened the window and scaled the wall blocking my view of the singing bird beyond, I would have done that there and then. Cell windows, however, are not made to be opened and there was no way I could climb through them to get to the wall a few inches away. But I could hear that bird singing for me, singing in celebration of my victory.

The heaviness that weighed me down in my indecision washes away and with ease I hoist my light, oh so light body up onto the toilet pot, gripping the grid of the window immediately above as I press my burning ear against the tiny square wires, trying to draw that sweet melody into the grey cell with me.

My mind returns to the court in time to hear the judge announce their acquittal. They are free to go. A weight rolls off my shoulders.

There are hugs all around.

One day when you are big and we are free, I will tell you the whole story, I say silently. That's a promise, Ruschka.

For now the story is stored in my mind, my little baby.

I hold her arm lightly as I guide her tiny hand through the sleeve of the matinee jacket. Over the white leggings are the two apple-green booties my comrade Zora hand-knitted. I tie the fine ribbons underneath her chin to secure the delicately worked cap and lay the shawl across the bed in readiness for the visit to her father. I always dress Ruschka beautifully on the odd occasion we are fortunate to see her dad.

She is not big enough to sit up in a baby seat in the car, so I lay her down in the carry-cot on the back seat and throw the apple-green shawl with its finely threaded ribbons lightly over her.

On the lonely road to her dad, zig-zag, zig-zag the whole way, it all floods back and silently I share with her the story the top brass of the security police would die to know.

Ruschka, it all began a month after you lodged your determined self in my womb. A man by the name of Joe Adam came to see your dad. He is an activist in the United Democratic Front (UDF) and was also in hiding like your dad and I. He said Mrs Mandela had come to another UDF activist by the name of Cheryl Carolus to say that she expected Madiba to be released soon. The Commonwealth was sending an Eminent Person's Group (EPG) to the country in January and they would meet with Madiba. He could either be released before or after that. Mrs Mandela said the problem was that we needed to prepare to welcome him and that this responsibility would fall on the Western Cape. Cheryl sent Joe to try and find your dad because, as you know, he is a very good organiser and has initiated many campaigns.

Your dad suggested to Joe that we consider making thousands of flags to be stored in every town in anticipation of the release.

The logic was that even if they banned gatherings or restricted Mandela in any way, it would be difficult for the state to prevent thousands of people from hoisting flags in the cities and rural towns.

Your dad discussed this with me and we realised that it would be impossible to depend on the comrades in Mitchells Plain to sew thousands of flags. Usually your dad's friend, Veronica Simmers, was the one we relied on to stitch the flag for meetings and other events. But one little sewing machine and one seamstress is not what we needed here. We had to do this in a factory. I scanned through the names of various factory owners in my head and then I remembered Fuad Carlie. I went to see him and discovered that he no longer owned a factory but was wholesaling clothes to small shops. But Fuad said he would come up with a plan and he did not fail us.

Elizabeth brought a number of seamstresses together and we were up and away.

The material had to be dyed specially in green and gold. Black material was easier to buy. The women had to work all evening for five days. Unfortunately, on the fifth day, armed men with black hoods over their faces surrounded the factory. They rushed in and arrested everybody. Somebody must have given us away. We had our suspicions but we didn't know for certain who it was.

Two weeks later, your dad and I were held up in Athlone. For some reason the security police were expecting us in that side street. Guns were trained on us, like you see in the movies. Up against the car our hands went and a helicopter hovered above. Handcuffs on your dad, forced into a police van. Handcuffs on my wrists, abruptly ending my morning sickness.

By the time we were released two months later, Madiba was still in prison and our hopes were waning. A few weeks later, our hopes were dashed when the Defence Force attacked ANC targets in Botswana, Zimbabwe and Zambia. They went in with their military planes the day before the EPG was due to see Mandela for a second time. We knew this was a signal that P W Botha was not interested in negotiation but wanted war. And war we now have on our hands, my dearest little baby.

One day when I tell you this story again, the war will have ended, Madiba will be home and we will be together as a family. I firmly believe this and it is only this idea that provides the energy to fuel my worn-out body.

At the red traffic light, I move the rear-view mirror so that I can catch a glimpse of my comrade's handiwork, so pleasing to tense eyes constantly on the look-out for suspicious cars. The shawl has slipped off the carry-cot, exposing your strong legs pulling first the one, then the other apple-green-bootied foot along the clown patterned cot blanket.

CHAPTER SIX

Ruschka snuggles into her plump padded body and ignores me. I look at the two of them and know that I have found the right substitute mother for my child.

Mozena Martin is a big woman with a warm smile. Our age difference is not that great but she has had three children and is an experienced mother. I am back at my mom's in Wynberg but I thought it would be unfair to leave my six-month-old baby in her care while I go to work. It is great, though, that she will be in the house and at hand to supervise Ruschka's other mother.

I am happy to finally meet her. She is from Wynberg, a few streets up from where I live. Her largeness wafts a certain magical assurance into my life. Ruschka clearly prefers her lap to mine. By comparison, I have no lap. Just bony legs, emaciated by a childhood tuberculosis. Considering Ruschka's reaction, a full breast and a well-padded stomach are far more desirable than the slender boniness elevated in the media as the preferred female form.

It is with a great sense of ease that I kiss my child goodbye and clamber into my car for my first day back at work. It's a new year with new beginnings. Motherhood is forcing adjustments that propel Ruschka's message – handle with care – to the forefront of my mind.

I am no longer a single young woman able to follow her whim. It is a funny state to be in, I think as I navigate the heavy morning traffic on the road to Bellville. I had never considered the change her presence would bring to my life. Some time long gone by when I was a university student, I had the idea that I would not get married nor have children. My attitude was that there were far too many hungry children in the world in need of care and that I would adopt some of them instead of adding to the world's problems. So I was not going to marry, nor produce children; I would instead be of service to my country and the world. Not exactly a nun. But something along those lines. Although I must say celibacy was never quite on the agenda.

Groups of students are gathered at the traffic light in the distance, waiting to be offered a lift. I stop and three jump in at the back and one in front.

I am not very chatty this morning and prefer to be immersed in my own thoughts. My mind goes back to how hugely surprised I was when I found my body taking over and flowing with the natural urges of all time, declaring readiness for procreation. And it happened at the worst possible time. I had been married for about two years and the country was in a state of emergency. I was homeless, in hiding with my husband, helping organise the resistance wherever I could. By any standards, this could be described as the worst possible time to have a child. Yet let no one say it was a mistake. We planned it. We wanted it and I deliberately stopped taking the contraception pill in September 1985. By October, I was pregnant. Well, my mother had six and after my first, I was left with the distinct impression that I was made to have six as well. There were no complications. I required very little medical attention during my pregnancy and I was on my feet immediately afterwards.

All quite crazy in retrospect but that was how it was.

By the time Ruschka was four months old, I was standing in the dock again, this time charged with obstructing Mostert in the course of his duty. I conducted my own defence, lost and was sentenced to three months suspended for three years. I needed to change course, to find some way to support my child and feel supported in return.

Jakes Gerwel's appointment as rector of the University of the Western Cape was like a godsend. I did not know him personally but Moegsien Williams, an old friend, was working at UWC as spokesperson for Dr Richard Van der Ross, the out-going rector. Moegsien was getting ready to take over the editorship of *South*, an alternative newspaper in the Cape, and somebody was needed to take his place.

"Go and see Jakes," said Moegsien. "He needs somebody to work for him."

I trotted along, determined to make a good impression. I felt in a precarious position, with a husband in hiding, a five-month-old baby and no job. I was always fiercely independent and reluctant to sponge off my parents from quite a young age. I wanted work that at least allowed me to earn more than the R300-odd a month we got at the union. Not only did my child depend on me, but also calls for help were coming from a number of activists unable to earn while they hid away to avoid arrest.

A tall secretary with green eyes and light-brown face showed me smilingly into his office. I had seen the professor on one or two public platforms in 1980 and 1981 when I was reporting for the *Cape Times* but it was always at a distance. He was known for his Afrikaans writing, and also his left-wing philosophical pronouncements. In front of me, stretching out his hand and leading me to a comfortable chair was a man of medium build, his frizzy hair neatly shaped into a cushion-like Afro, the hairstyle of the time.

"I cannot tell you how glad I am that you have walked through this door," he said. "I did not know what I was going to do when Moegsien left."

As I arrive at UWC for my first day of work, I am aware that I am about to go into a very different environment. I have no idea what awaits me but am conscious of this institution's rich history of resistance politics.

It was established in 1963 as a separate university for Coloured people, fitting into the apartheid plan of creating separate spaces for different racial groups. It became the hub of the Black Consciousness movement in the mid-70s, producing layers of leaders committed to the anti-apartheid struggle inside and outside the country.

The students hop out as soon as I am parked, effusively thanking me. I watch them as they walk away and cannot help thinking how young they look. It takes me a few minutes to connect with the notion that that was me ten years ago.

The tall secretary with the green eyes ushers Moegsien and myself into Jakes's office. She sets a tray of tea and biscuits on the desk in front of us. Moegsien says he will be in and out for another three months as he slowly moves over to *South*. Jakes gives me some idea of what his plans are for the university. I am not keen to be a spokesperson, I say. I am happiest writing and producing publications. But I am happy to do a bit of both.

After the meeting, Moegsien takes me to a tiny little office just big enough for one desk, two chairs and a bookshelf to be shared by us for the next few weeks.

We tour the campus and I discover a variety of people who constitute the engine of this apartheid machine that Jakes believes he can transform into a non-racial institution.

By the time I arrive home, Ruschka is fast asleep in my nephew Khalil's old steel-rimmed cot. I had to go to a women's meeting before coming home from work. My mom has sent our other mother home and the house is quiet. I know Ruschka will sleep through. I have to be content with cuddling her in the morning. I stand quietly next to her cot and gaze at her, satisfied that she is breathing. My mom has advised me not to feed her at night but offer her a water bottle if she wakes up. "It won't be worth it for her to wake up for water," says my experienced mother. "You will see, she will then sleep through."

My new life as a mother was simplified a hundred-fold the day I decided to follow one person's advice. When Ruschka was born, I had felt bombarded by well-meaning friends and family. When the child cried, the one would say it's colic, give her some drops to stop the stomach cramps. Then the other would say she has wind. Sit her up straight and bash her on her back gently. How do you bash a baby on its back gently?

No, it's not colic. It's post-nasal drip. That's what she has.

It drove me mad. Until it dawned on me that I needed to choose one person and follow her advice in the main. What better person than my mother? I have seen some friends pore over books and try religiously to follow the instructions, and have concluded it was a good decision to be guided by somebody who had successfully raised half-a-dozen of her own.

My life became much easier then. I listened to everybody but did what my mother said. A bottle with strained oats and condensed milk may not have been the most scientific option but it did the trick when Ruschka wailed after trying to suck the thin gruel from my useless breasts. When she was two months old, I had to give up and settle for the bottle.

I am relieved to see the diaper bag neatly stacked with soft folded cloths, ready for use first thing in the morning. Designed in the shape of a long dress, it hangs on the knob of the cupboard beside the cot, confirming that our other mother is naturally tidy. I feel she is a wand I can wave as I battle to learn to be a parent in the midst of a war for our nationhood.

I resist bending down to touch Ruschka's forehead with my lips. All I need is for her to wake up and demand my attention. I gently move the soft flannel blanket over her small shoulders before clambering into the single bed beside the cot.

My body is dead tired but happy as I fall into a deep sleep.

CHAPTER SEVEN

It's early Saturday morning and I leave Ruschka at home because I sense that today is going to be hard. Reaching Bonteheuwel, a sprawling township on the Cape Flats, takes less than twenty minutes from my home in Wynberg. I park my car on the sandy sidewalk and walk towards the small council house belonging to Ivy Kriel. Activists are dotted all along the fence in front of the house and in the small barren space meant for a garden, now filled with plastic chairs. I pass through them, nodding a silent greeting which they return. Those who are speaking to one another are whispering.

I join the line of family members as they slowly file past the body. Ashley Kriel is lying flat on his back in the coffin in the middle of the tiny room. There is barely space to move. And then I see his face. I look but cannot see. Yet, I do see. His forehead is swollen. His eyes are closed. A deep gash leaping out of his forehead has been stitched up by the coroner. The dark curls are brushed back. In that split second, my eyes blur and I feel my knees bending. A sharp pain shoots through my chest. A comrade hoists me up under my arms, steadying me. I am helped up the narrow steps to a bedroom upstairs where I find Ashley's sister Melanie. We are both crying.

I know that I had to look at him some time. I was reluctant because I wanted to remember him as I knew him. But it would have been strange for me not to be part of the family ritual. Melanie, unlike her sister Michelle, is unable to function. While twenty-four-year-old Michelle is in the kitchen below helping visitors to the family home, her sister, sedated the night before, cannot stop crying.

It was Michelle who had called me a week ago at UWC and given me the news: "Zubeida, the police have shot Ashley. They took me to see his body in the morgue this afternoon. Please tell everybody." I became icy cold. As if a winter chill had descended on my office. I cut out, suppressing all emotions.

"Where is your mother? Don't worry, I'll be there as soon as I can."

I had left work immediately, thinking about the need to form a funeral committee, finding lawyers to investigate the killing, raising the money to help the family. There was no time to deal with emotions. Organising often became a way of coping with horrors that we dealt with daily. We had to be strong for the family, for the community, hiding how completely shattered we were.

I was aware that Ashley had left the country about a year after his final school exams. Some had tried to dissuade him but he was angry. He and his friends in Bonteheuwel were shot at with birdshot and beaten whenever they tried to organise meetings at their school. He wanted to be equipped to fight back and had decided the only way was to be armed himself. He left the country at the end of 1985 and joined the military wing of the ANC, Umkhonto we Sizwe.

I regret now that I looked at his face this morning. Unknown to many of us, he was sent back after being trained and had been living at a house in Hazendal, a small working class, Coloured suburb near Athlone. I would have preferred remembering him as I knew him.

I used to watch him closely when he arose to address the crowds at meetings of the United Democratic Front. I was never quite sure whether it was his political rhetoric or his personal charisma that set the crowd off. "Viva Ashley, Viva! Long live, long live!"

> Igama lama Ashley Kriel, malibongwe.
> Igama lama Ashley Kriel, malibongwe."
> (The name of Ashley Kriel, let it be praised.
> The name of Ashley Kriel, let it be praised.)

He had this way of raising his arm alongside his ear when he shouted: "Amandla!" (Power!). To which the crowd responded tumultously: "Ngawethu!" (To the people!) All speakers ended their speeches with these words. But not all raised their right arm as Ashley did. Some right arms were pushed forward diagonally with their fists clenched. Other arms were bent at the elbow at a kind of right angle to the shoulder. Ashley's arm was always straight in the air with four fingers clenched in a fist and the thumb extended, the ANC's power salute.

The extension of his arm elongated his body, giving him a new kind of height which added a further dimension to his defiant words. I could see the young women comrades in the audience tantalised by his charm. Although the sexual appeal would have been dominant amongst the women, he had his male admirers too. The combination of personal charm and political commitment made him a youth leader of great attraction.

He was the Che Guevara of the Cape Flats. Long, tapered face with a mop of curly black hair. A lean, slender body dressed in khaki shirt and black beret. We were all proud, very proud of him.

When Ashley came to ask if he could stay with me for his final school year, I was happy to have him. We were able to provide him with comfortable study space so that he could do the best that he was able to.

In a different time, he may have been the local Don Juan. But he grew into his teens just when the schools' protest erupted in the Western Cape. With the formation of the United Democratic Front (UDF), one of our veteran youth organisers, Cecyl Esau, was quick to identify Ashley as the one who could help bring the youth of his township together to form a branch of the Cape Youth Congress.

While all of us who had organised and mobilised people against apartheid developed a special relationship during those years, it did not always mature into full-blown love. Ashley was one of the few who evoked that unreserved emotion. He was loved not only by his family but also by many of us who saw in him the embodiment of all our hopes. He was young, from an impoverished background, but held his own on public platforms with veteran leaders such as Alan Boesak and Oscar Mpetha.

The previous week, as part of the funeral committee, it had been one of my jobs to piece together the scant information that we had about the circumstances surrounding his death. Mourning in that crowded little house where his body lay, I relived the painful night when I sat down to prepare a fact file for the press.

I have waited for Ruschka to sleep so that I can be undisturbed as I compile my notes into a coherent whole. When the night is mine, the words come easily and I stop only intermittently when two of the metal arms of the typewriter with letters e and r get entangled. With my forefinger, I lightly unhook the one arm from the other. They slide into place on the keyboard and I resume my typing:

Ashley Kriel was alone when he died. Salma Ismail, the schoolteacher with whom he boarded, was at work. Her younger brother Imtiaz Ismail had taken their vacuum cleaner for repairs. They knew Ashley as "James".

> In a prepared statement this week, police said he died from a bullet fired from his own weapon during a scuffle with two policemen who had tried to disarm and arrest him at the Athlone house.

The statement does not explain why Ashley was wearing handcuffs as claimed by Imtiaz Ismail who returned from his errand about 1.30 p.m.

Imtiaz's witness is as follows:
"As I pulled into the driveway, three or four plain-clothes policemen told me to stop. I switched off the car. They told me and the friend with me to stand with our hands against the car and they searched us.

"I then walked around the back of the house with the policeman following me. I saw James lying on his side. There was blood on his forehead. His arms were stretched out in front of him and he was wearing handcuffs.

"The police were looking for more handcuffs but could not find any. They took the handcuffs off James and put them on me.

"I asked one policeman what was wrong with James and he told me: 'Hy is doodgeskiet omdat hy 'n terroris is.' (He was shot dead because he was a terrorist.)"

I blot out Ashley's face as I write and write, finally signing off the sheet as issued by the Ashley Kriel Funeral Committee.

The next day, we hand out the fact sheet to journalists at a press conference with an addendum: "The above information will be used by the *Weekly Mail* this week. Journalists are free to make use of any information since it is not possible to bring family members and others together here at this press conference."

A further information sheet has all the details of the funeral programme for the following day. We could not have imagined how complex our funeral plans were to become.

I pull myself together and help Melanie move down the steps so that she can follow her brother's coffin out of the house. His body is placed inside the waiting hearse. We get into our cars and slowly file into line so that the procession can move in an orderly fashion towards the New Apostolic Church.

It is a dark grey winter's day, as if the skies reflect the sombreness of the mourners. We hope it will not rain and deter people from gathering on the sports field as planned.

At the church, we see the armoured vehicles parked all around. Casspirs with armed men peering from their open doors greet fearful mourners as they file into the church. Many of us are accustomed to this display of force but for the average member of the New Apostolic Church, this is not something they generally encounter when they attend Sunday services.

I can see the fear on peoples' faces. They are quiet and very nervous. The proceedings are brief. Ashley's uncle speaks. The priest makes some general biblical commentary, his blandness offensive to the activists.

I scan the pews: women in their black dresses or suits with black hats or lace scarves. Men with their hats in their hands resting on the laps of their black pants.

They are part of a conservative religious community and they love Ivy. She had listened to the deacons as best she could when they explained the detail of the service. She knew they were not excited about welcoming the many khaki-clad youth who were determined to demonstrate wearing the volunteer uniform of the ANC.

She cared deeply for her son but she never cared for his involvement in politics. She never quite understood it. And now it had brought about his death, justifying her opposition to his involvement. He was the one she had relied on when she became ill. He was the one whom she had hoped would care for her when she became old.

She has a weak heart and when she could not work, when Ashley was fourteen, she reluctantly allowed him to go out in the middle of the night to sell the local daily Afrikaans newspaper, *Die Burger*. She and her daughters waited for him at 5 a.m. to take the few cents he earned for the day to buy bread. Then she would make him as comfortable as possible for his short sleep before he had to wake up again and ready himself for school.

The crowd surges towards the door at the end of the service, then suddenly retreats.

"What's going on?" I ask.

Before anybody can answer, I smell it – the pungent ammonia stinging the air floating through the open church door. "Oh my God, they are shooting!" shouts a mourner.

The armed men stationed outside the church shoot rounds of teargas at the pallbearers as they descend the steps. The activists take over and run with the coffin all the way to a second church to get it away from the gas overpowering the mourners.

As I pass through the door and out into the hazy daylight, I see the coffin dancing grimly on the shoulders of the young men moving rapidly down the streets. I cringe, thinking of Ashley's battered body bashing up against the coffin sides as different waves of comrades pass the casket on like a baton in a relay and run with it as fast as they can.

There is little point in trying to get to my car. Some churchgoers are in a hurry to get home as quickly as they can. The only way many of us can maintain our dignity is to walk through the mass of armed men circling the church and follow the body on foot. Fleetingly, I imagine that today is the day I will die. Ruschka will be looked after. I do not have to worry. I have always wondered when it will come, but today all the elements are in place. A helicopter hovers directly above us in the overcast sky. Rows of yellow riot vehicles are backed up by masked men who train their automatic weapons on us. All along the road, sharpshooters are crouched on the rooftops of the small Bonteheuwel dwellings, prepared for retaliatory action from the ANC's military wing, Umkhonto we Sizwe (MK). We know such an offensive would never come on the streets of Bonteheuwel, crowded with civilians. The commander-in-chief, Chris Hani, would never sanction such action. There is talk that he had taken a special liking to Ashley and that he had personally given the go-ahead for him to be sent back into the country. In these times, it is not always possible to distinguish between speculation and fact.

I gather from the police reaction that they too must have believed that Chris had a direct interest in this fatality. Although I have never met him, I feel he is the one person we can rely on to fight back against the might of the apartheid military machine. Yet it would have made no sense for MK to plan anything at the funeral to endanger ordinary people. Public demonstrations or funerals are seldom occasions for military activity. They are used rather for mobilisation of communities and their radicalisation, providing fertile soil for underground military activities.

Arriving at the Anglican Church, the funeral committee quickly realises that any plans to move the funeral onto the field would be too dangerous. We confer with Archbishop Desmond Tutu, the Reverend Alan Boesak and Moulana Faried Essack and decide to merge the programme planned for the field and the one for the church. The church service becomes a mass rally and the mass rally becomes a church service.

Out comes the ANC flag to be draped over the coffin. Hymns merge into freedom songs and freedom songs into hymns. Tears become laughter and laughter becomes tears. Both Tutu and Boesak poke fun at the police, creating a levity essential to lowering the mood of anger.

Outside the church, Ashley's mother remains seated in the family car. It has all become too much for her and she refuses to participate in the second service. I am torn between going to persuade her to come in and just letting her be. Knowing her deep sadness and how conflicted she felt, I decide it's best to just let her be.

She has given us her heart in the beautiful body of her son. It is unfair to expect her to give us her own body to appease our broken hearts.

Thinking about her alone in the car outside, I remember the story she once told me about the time before Ashley disappeared. He had come home one night and slipped his arms lovingly around her waist, presenting her with a chocolate to ease the tension which had built up between them over his activities.

With his arm around her waist, they had sat close together sharing the chocolate. He had a way about him that made everything right for her and the chocolate helped work the magic.

A few days later he asked her for money to pay the shopkeeper on the corner. When she wanted to know what it was for he said: "Dit is vir die chocolate wat ek vir ma gekoop het." (For the chocolate I bought you, mom.)

I smile when I remember her laughter that day long before his death.

The service is over and Archbishop Tutu, Allan Boesak and Faried Essack follow the black-, green- and gold-draped coffin out of the church towards the parked hearse. The police had earlier placed restrictions on the funeral, forbidding the display of the ANC flag. As the pallbearers fit the coffin into the hearse, the head of the riot police, Major Dolf Odendaal makes a dash for the flag. He tries to drag it off the hearse. He pulls on one side and the pallbearers, trying to set the coffin down, pull on the other. Moulana Faried Essack steps into the fray and grabs the flag, making it impossible for Odendaal to pull it off. Ivy watches this undignified tussle over her son's stiff body. The pallbearers, helped by the Muslim imām, manage to slide the coffin into the vehicle and slam the door shut.

The hearse bolts forward like a frightened horse, leaving the family and mourners gaping in astonishment. The driver does not slow down but gallops apace while we dash to find vehicles to follow the procession. For a moment, I wonder how on earth I would have managed if I had brought Ruschka into this chaos. Then I jump into a friend's car and we drive down the main road in Bonteheuwel into Vanguard Drive. The cortege is out of sight. Instead we see rows of masked armed riot police lining the street all the way to the cemetery in Maitland. It is a good ten kilometres from the church. Cars are piled up, mourners mixed with the daily traffic along the busy industrial road.

A handful of people make it to the graveyard to lower Ashley to his final resting-place. When we arrive, the police block our entry at the gates. I am hysterical, shouting, pushing. Ashley did not deserve to be buried this way. He did not deserve to be buried this way. He was the handsome one, the much-loved one, and the charming one whom they deprived us of even in his death. It's so hard to imagine what logic drives their punitive behaviour. It is completely beyond me why they do not want us to say our last goodbyes. Grieving angry faces stamped with the same bewilderment throng around me.

A fleeting image of a man smiling broadly passes through my mind. Chris Hani, commander-in-chief of MK. His muscles bulge through his khaki shirt. His large forehead dominates his caramel-coloured face. He smiles at me with his characteristic broad grin captured in a photograph stealthily circulated amongst comrades and stored in my memory. That ready smile set in a face ringed by a cushion of soft steely hair. The man who has the arms to protect us. We need help, Chris. We need you.

A sombre group of family and friends meet at a church hall in Bonteheuwel for the funeral meal. Local cooks have prepared huge pots of minced meat curry and rice and dish generous helpings onto our cardboard plates. We pull up our chairs informally into circles, trying to make light of the day's events. "Well, we are all alive," says one comrade. "This food is just what I needed," says another.

The warmth of the food eases my tension and I am grateful to be alive. It is so hard to think of Ashley. We prefer to laugh about the fight over the flag. What a sight it had been. The clergy on one side, the police on the other and the flag in between.

A young girl runs into the hall shouting: "Die boere is hier buite!" (The police are outside.)

"Lock the doors?" "But why?" "What do they want now?" Questions ripple through the crowd. Some leave the hall. As they do, the first canister whizzes past our heads, emitting the sickly white teargas. Everybody starts running. Some close the doors in panic. Some try to crawl under tables. Others double over to vomit.

For some unknown reason, I decide to run onto the stage. But there is no place to hide. The gas is floating across the hall. My chest is tightening. At the back of the stage, people are trying to open the back door. They are pulling and banging on it. I want to help the old woman in front of me as she falls to the ground but I cannot because it feels like my lungs are about to explode. I must find air.

I press up against the back of the stage wall to hide and die without being beaten. I am expecting the police to come flooding into the hall waving their batons and guns. We are trapped and the pain in my chest is growing sharper. It is as if my lungs are blowing up like balloons about to burst through my chest. I have to move or go down like the elderly woman on the floor in front of me. Then I hear the back door open. Some young comrades have managed to open it and I go tumbling down the ramp into air. In the rush to breathe, I had tripped and fallen from the confines of the gas-filled hall. I lay on my back staring up at the rain-laden clouds, thankful to be alive.

CHAPTER EIGHT

I am sweating. I see the man coming towards me. He is tall with deep blue eyes and black hair. He is the one who said he was hung upside down from a tree in East Africa during the war against the Mau-Mau. I do not know why he was there in the first place but that's what he told me. He is a police captain. I cannot let him hit me again. He is going to slam me into the wall like he did a minute ago. He is coming towards me. I look around and see a gun lying on the table behind me. I grab the gun. My hand is completely still. I shoot once, twice, three times. He is flying through the air, blood pouring from his chest. I stand still with the gun in my hand.

Then my body shakes, my eyes open and I feel my soaked vest against the damp sheet. It's Saturday night and I had the same dream last night. Oh my God, help! It's coming back, that dream of eight years ago. Night after night, it haunted me in the days after my release from detention. And suddenly it vanished. Now it's coming back. Why is it coming back? That was then. This is now. It all happened so long ago. The detention. The feelings of terror. I try to go back to sleep but cannot.

It's Sunday morning and Ruschka needs my attention. Her morning bath, a clean nappy to be pinned on, clean clothes that Mozena has washed and ironed in the week. Then mixing the cereal into the bowl. I cannot hear her. I mix the cereal into the bowl. I move the spoon from the bowl towards her mouth. I hear her. Her gurgles are too loud. They fill my head. They are very loud. I cannot stand them. "Dad, can you play with Ruschka? Dad, can you take Ruschka with you this morning?" I say desperately.

"Are you feeling alright?" my dad asks.

"I just did not sleep well," I say. I don't want to scare him.

Ruschka needs lunch. She needs supper. It's not easy being a mother. Suddenly you are responsible for another being on a twenty-four-hour basis. Another person who is completely dependent on you.

Soon she will sleep. I don't have to prepare for work tomorrow. I have taken leave to coincide with the end of the first-term holidays. What a relief it is to have completed all the work I had promised Jakes I would do. We had decided to produce a special edition of the *UWC NEWS* for all parents to keep them informed of the university's stance on the then state president F W de Klerk's measures that sought to curb political expression on campus. UWC, together with UCT, had taken De Klerk to the Supreme Court asking that the measures be set aside, both for being *ultra vires* and for vagueness. A full bench of the Supreme Court ruled in our favour on all counts, declaring those measures invalid.

But then came the banning of seventeen organisations, making it impossible for the South African National Students Congress (SANSCO) and the National Education Crisis Committee (NECC), to operate on campus. The restrictions came just weeks after the state crushed our efforts to organise a welcome home rally for Govan Mbeki, the first political leader to be released after spending twenty-five years on Robben Island. The rally was banned and the grey-haired giant, affectionately known as Oom Gov, was confined to his home in New Brighton.

Each time we make a gain, the state gallops through us like a wild horse flattening the achievement.

I have to believe that this is the wildness of a horse in its dying throes. Any other thought is too overwhelming. To think they would destroy everything that we have built and that we would not be able to recover is a notion I cannot entertain for a second.

Alone with my thoughts, I am like a ship in the vortex of the hot and cold currents swishing wildly at Cape Point. No sooner do the warm waters wash across my hull, soothing a battered body, than the cold waters dash the fleeting sense of hope.

As I sit quietly next to Ruschka, her eyes slowly drooping closed, the memory of the day I met Oom Gov comes back to me.

A tall man reclining against the hospital pillows. He sits up as I step forward to greet him. "So lovely to meet you, so lovely," he says. He holds my small hand in his large rough palm, gripping it firmly as he chuckles. I am conscious that there are a number of people who want to step up to the bed to greet him. This is his first visit to Cape Town since his release. He has been granted permission to come for medical attention to Groote Schuur Hospital. Despite his cotton pyjamas, he does not appear less forceful than the night we first saw him on television. Then he was dressed in a silver-grey suit, a red tie and white shirt with his white mop of hair in stark contrast to his dark-brown face. He declared to the world that imprisonment had not deterred him from his commitment to communism.

53

He is aware that I had shared the coordination of the reception committee that had hoped to formally welcome him to Cape Town. For weeks,
teams of activists had worked from morning till night to claw back some
public space to express ourselves. Momentarily the state had hesitated. Then
the vacillation ended and the crack-down had come like a ton of bricks. The
local magistrate had refused permission for us to hold a rally and the justice minister had banned Oom Gov.

I hand him a lapel button with his picture superimposed on a background of black, green and gold. We had distributed thousands of buttons,
posters and sweaters displaying his picture in preparation for the public
rally. He seems to sense that I am bruised. "You have done well," he says.
"Don't worry."

As I step back to allow others to greet him, I am worried. Very worried.

The memory of that sense of worry now overwhelms me as I watch over
Ruschka whose breathing is slow and even. I am past the warm oceans,
plunging into the icy cold current that is gaining strength and pushing me
off course.

With a one-year-old child, a husband in hiding, a full-time job and serving as treasurer of the United Women's Congress, there is no energy left to
deal with further crises. I sit on the bed and am still. I have nothing to do.
My child is asleep. I will be away from work for two weeks. My time is my
own.

It's frightening to think of sleep. What if the nightmare comes again? I
don't want to be reminded of the terror I felt. I prefer blocking out the feeling, blocking it off, barricading myself against memory. I reach for a book,
turn the pages and try to read. After five minutes, I give up. I cannot concentrate. I have not been able to for weeks now.

Perhaps watching television will be simpler. I walk to the lounge and flick
on the screen. I need to relax. Music on one channel, news? Oh, not news.
I cannot bear it. The music then. I do not last a minute. It's too noisy. The
sounds are echoing in my head. They are ringing in my head. I go back to
my room. I have been dead, not really feeling anything. Now I am feeling
something. It is as if my head is caving in. The pressure is strong on the
top of my head. I know there is something wrong. Am I losing my mind?
Am I having a nervous breakdown? Is this how it is to have a nervous
breakdown?

I need help and can only think of one person. Ramsay Karelse, the psychiatrist who was a board member of *Grassroots*, the community newspaper we had so successfully organised for all of the eighties.

I call him.

"Ramsay, I think I am having a nervous breakdown." I describe how I feel.

"Come and see me first thing in the morning. I am fully booked but just come."

I cannot get into the car the next morning and ask my dad to take me to the doctor. My legs feel weak. My parents are shocked and worried that I want to see a psychiatrist but my dad takes me and Ramsay sees me immediately. Afterwards he asks his assistant to call my dad into the consulting room.

"Mr Jaffer, Zubeida is suffering from a major depression and post-traumatic stress disorder," he says. "Something happens that triggers off a part of her memory," says Ramsay, "and she has a sudden emotional reaction that is unexpected. It will get less and less over time, but she has been under too much pressure and I think she should be allowed to rest as much as possible," he says.

"She won't be able to rest at home, because the police are in and out," says my dad.

"Well, find a place for her to rest. She is not having a nervous breakdown but she could have one if she does not rest. I have to put her off work for a month. She will not be able to look after her child or anybody else. The tablets I am going to give her are going to make her sleep most of the time."

I am stubborn and also needy. I need to be with my husband so I join him where he is hiding. But it is not a good place to be because of the level of tension. He is tense, I am tense, our host is tense, not knowing what to expect. We cannot stay anywhere for more than a few days. I am asleep most of the time. It's a kind of blurred existence. I am not aware of anything much. I wake up to eat, take my tablets and relieve myself. The tablets make it difficult for me to walk. I drop onto the bed and sleep again.

Elaborate arrangements are made so that I can see Ruschka. I am happy to see her but not very aware of her. She is rolling on me, on the bed but I cannot feel her. Now she is here, then she is not. I cannot laugh or cry. I am like a zombie, drugged into a hazy existence.

After two weeks, I am back at my parents' home in Wynberg. Jakes comes to see me. I explain that I cannot function. That I need more time. "Take as much time as you need," says Jakes. "Just get better."

55

I am so relieved that he understands. I am slowly clawing my way back into the outside world where I have to be ready to face aggression. Inside me, my world is fearful and disjointed. I am unsure whether my mind will torture me again once the tablets are decreased.

Ramsay and I talk. He cannot get me to delve inside. I don't want to talk about my experience of torture. I don't want to remember the humilation I felt when I gave them the names of friends and a colleague. I don't want to remember the image of grey dandruff-covered hair ringing a ghost-like face that I saw by chance in a mirror after days of interrogation.

That was me eight years ago, an unrecognisable apparition quickly disappearing. I prefer to worry about the army parading up and down our streets, barging into our homes, our mosques, shooting people. I cannot relax. He recommends gym and lots of sleep and slow measured eating. I have the habit of eating very quickly. There is always a meeting to rush to, some drama to attend to. It has been like this for nearly ten years. I am exhausted and overwhelmed. There is so much, there has been so much. I tell Ramsay the story of the first time, in 1980, when children at a Hanover Park High School had contacted me at the *Cape Times*. I remember the day as clearly as if it was just yesterday.

I am at my desk at the *Cape Times*. It is Sunday morning and Sundays are usually quiet news days. I had joined the *Cape Times* in February 1980 after having spent a few weeks at the *Rand Daily Mail* in Johannesburg. The telephone rings on my desk and the person introduces himself as Zackie Achmat, a community worker at the mosque in Hanover Park.

He has seen my name in the paper and wants me to come to Broad Road in Wynberg in the afternoon. "We are organising a protest at the Coloured Affairs," he says. "Pupils at Crystal Senior Secondary School are opposed to their principal and the poor facilities and are taking action," he says.

Broad Road separates Wynberg from Kenilworth. It is perhaps appropriate that the Coloured Affairs Department is on that road which marks the end of our area, designated coloured under apartheid, and Kenilworth, designated white. All of us, for different reasons, resent that building, which is a daily reminder of our status in this country.

It is to this institution that I had had to direct my application for special permission to attend the university of my choice. They had eventually sent me the permit, part of which read as follows: "In terms of the Extension of University Education Act, 1959 as amended by section 1 of Act 29 of 1971, the Minister of Coloured Relations and Rehoboth Affairs has approved that Miss Z Jaffer may be enrolled as a student at the University of Cape Town for the year 1975 for study of the BA degree which must include the following subject: Comparative African Government and Law.

We who were not white could only attend the University of Cape Town if we dug out some obscure subject not offered at the University of the Western Cape specially established for us.

The *Cape Times* car with myself and a photographer in it pass under the railway bridge and into Broad Road. The road is quiet, not unusual for a Sunday afternoon. There is no sign of protesters in the distance.

We slow down as we come to the offensive building and then I see the protest. The pupils have secretly tied huge placards onto the wire fence surrounding the Coloured Affairs Department, voicing their objections to conditions at their school.

We take the pictures. I do the story. It appears in the *Cape Times* the next morning, giving the first indication of the major upheavals we are about to face in the coming months. Zackie calls again and then others call. I have to eat as quickly as I can. There is just too little time in one day. Gobble, gobble, gobble. On to the next phone call, interview, meeting. Gobble, gobble. Soon all the schools are involved in the protests, then the universities. At the same time, the meat workers go on strike and commuters boycott the buses, prompting the detention of hordes of activists. More work for those of us left behind. Gobble, gobble. Rush. Rush.

"You must try to slow down your life," says Ramsay.

I have no idea how I am going to do this because I am so used to the tempo. But I know I am in serious trouble. I cannot afford to get those nightmares again. They constrict my heart, making me unable to think, to reason. I am relieved that the tablets have made them go away, forcing them somewhere into my subconscious.

The days go by and I am able to feed Ruschka. I mash the pumpkin, add a sliver of butter and mix it with the mashed potatoes. She is not one of those children who one needs to coax to eat. She eats heartily, plays heartily and sleeps heartily. I thank God every day. It was only in the first three months, when she developed colic, that I battled to understand what to do.

I reach the stage where I have the strength to bathe her. I undress her, sit her down in the warm water and soap her firm body with a soft white cloth. In the baby bath, she fiddles with a rubber teething ring and asks me for her little yellow rubber duck.

"He can swim, mummy," she says as she moves the little duck through the bath water.

I warm the towel over the heater and lay it on the single bed in the room that we occupy. Her third winter comes as she is about to turn two and the evenings are cold in the Cape. I lift her from the bath and onto the warm towel, fluffing her skin dry with gentle round movements of my hands.

Into warm clothes and ready for the night and her last milk bottle.

I am so proud of myself that I have managed to bathe her without any help and that her joyful gurgle is no longer a loud noise but a dove cooing softly in my head.

CHAPTER NINE

I tiptoe through her room into mine. When the months became years, my father built an extra room on to the house so that Ruschka and I could have a room each. I hear her stir. I must have woken her as I came in. I look at her and see her sitting straight up in bed. The room is dark so I have to move closer to her to see if she is awake. Why is she sitting up so straight? Normally, if she wakes up she just keeps on lying with her eyes open. Is she dreaming? Her little face has a pensive expression.

"Sweetie pie!" I say, sitting down, ready to put my arms around her.

She looks at me very seriously and says: "Mom, is dad coming home?"

"Yes, sweetheart. Tomorrow."

She smiles, moves onto her back, pulls her bed-sheet under her chin and closes her eyes.

I am still not sure whether she has been fully conscious through this performance. The smile followed immediately by sleep pleases me though.

It has been a tough few days and Ruschka is aware that I am running around trying to help her father. Our lawyer Essa has informed the police that we are applying for a restraining order against them and they in turn have offered to make a number of concessions if Johnny hands himself over voluntarily. He will be appearing in court tomorrow.

We are up early and dress in light summer clothes. I put on Ruschka's prettiest dress and brush her dark curly hair carefully. Her cheeks are shining and flushed with excitement at the thought of flying into her dad's arms today. With my parents, we travel to the Goodwood Magistrate's Court, where Johnny is to appear.

His friend Rashid has hired a three-piece grey suit so that he is appropriately dressed for the court appearance. It will be the first time in three years that he will legally make an appearance in public. We see him as he ascends the stairwell under the court into the accused box. "Dada," shouts Ruschka. He is smiling. She is excited, moving around on my lap.

The last week has been a haze of drama. Now that I am here in court, knowing that he is about to come home, I do not regret the trauma of the past few days.

It all started when his colleague, Nabs Wessels, asked Johnny to come to her farewell party in Muizenberg. He was reluctant to go but she was a good friend and close comrade and he decided to take the chance to go to the Dora Falcke Centre across the road from Sunrise Beach in Muizenberg. The police must have been tipped off that he was there, because they came too, but as they sped up the sandy path towards the centre, he slipped out of a back window and into the dense seaside bushes.

Armed with machine guns, the policemen held up all the partygoers, who were from different churches in the Cape. When they realised that he was not amongst them, they combed the bushes along the beach. It was early evening and the sun had set. It was difficult for them to see anything so they fired shots into the dunes and into the bushes. He could see them though, and had taken off his shirt, his dark skin blending with the black bushes. Then one of the men stood on his hand. He managed not to move. They were all around him. He heard them consider setting fire to the bushes to smoke him out. Across the road at the farewell party, Nabs and others heard the gunfire but were under police-guard. There was nothing they could do. They expected a dead body and the flurry of organising a funeral. We had become so used to living from one funeral to another that the poet Don Matera said we had become a nation of pallbearers.

The cop moved his foot off Johnny's hand and walked on further. He heard them moving off slowly into the distance and remained lying in the same position. Later that night, when he could no longer hear anything, he crawled through the bushes all along the sand dunes to Mitchells Plain about ten kilometres away.

I was in my bed at home and had no idea of the drama. Nor did Ruschka. I tried not to tell her much for fear of disturbing her. The next day in the afternoon, Nabs arrived at my door after I returned from work. She haltingly told me the whole story and for me it was just too much. It was too close a shave. I could not believe that I only got to know about what had happened twenty-four hours later. My husband could have been dead and they did not want to tell me until they had some idea of whether he was dead or alive. A part of me was angry. I felt they should have come to tell me immediately. But then another part also felt that they had done their best to protect me under the circumstances and I appreciated that.

As the years have gone by it has become more and more difficult for us to see one another because the pressure has intensified. There are always cops sitting in cars outside our home. They not only sit there but also have been into neighbours' homes in the middle of the night, saying they think my husband is hiding there. Often they go into homes quite arbitrarily and the poor people don't know what has hit them. The next day, they will be at my mother's door telling their story. I can only think it is a way to prevent anybody in my immediate vicinity from helping us.

It is not only the people of Wynberg who have born the brunt of it: relatives of relatives do not have an easy time. My sister-in-law's poor brother, who had just come to wish my parents on Eid Day, was arrested a few days later in the early hours of the morning. He was accused of having me in his car with him on Eid Day. That was during the time we were in hiding in 1985 and the cops were looking for both of us.

Siraj was arrested at his home in the dead of the night, driven to my parents' home and other homes he had visited on Eid day. He was then frog-marched back to his own home after clearly being unable to provide the police with any answers. His father, Hoosain, in desperation prayed over a bottle of water for days and then came to our house to sprinkle the holy water across our front porch to prevent the police from crossing that line into our home. But holy water could not do the trick. They kept on crossing the threshold and barging in, week after week, month after month, year after year.

What gave me strength through these dark times were the many efforts of people on the periphery like Hoosain Bhai. Those who put their jobs on the line. Those who helped without seeking glory or any financial reward. People of all colours, creeds, shapes and sizes.

In a way it is a good thing that the incident happened in Muizenberg last week. It has helped bring three awful years to an end. The police have agreed not to oppose bail and have set it at R2 000 and not the original R5 000 they proposed. Essa has agreed to withdraw the application for a court order restraining the police from assaulting or harming Johnny in any way. He has extracted a number of concessions from them. They have agreed not to detain Johnny when he arrives at court and have dropped the requirement that he report to police daily or be confined to the Cape Town magisterial district. Instead, he has to report to the police weekly.

Johnny has spent the greater part of the past thirteen years under banning orders or in detention. If I add up the months he spent in detention without trial, it comes close to twenty. When we married he had just been released from Pollsmoor Prison for breaking his banning order pending an appeal against a twelve-month sentence.

In all the years, he never faced formal charges other than minor ones related to his banning order that restricted his movement and limited his interaction with others. While he was one of the key organisers of the UDF, the state prevented him from holding official positions. Now he is coming home and I cannot help wondering for how long or what shock next awaits us.

The court proceedings are at an end. We gather outside, waiting for his release. Essa has to pay the bail money and certain papers have to be signed. After about an hour, he comes through the court gates into the bright sunlight. Ruschka runs into his arms, clinging to her father as he clings to her. She is a big little girl who has not seen her daddy for weeks.

Nabs Wessels and her husband Chris, a Moravian minister, have invited us home for tea. Chris is ministering to a congregation in Elsies River not far from the Goodwood court. The media contingent follows us to their home and I observe Ruschka enjoying the constant clicks of cameras. It is strange for her to be with her father in the company of many people. Already nearly three years old, she only remembers ever seeing him alone or with the family members of the household where he was in hiding.

On the tables fresh cream cakes, cooldrinks and warm cups of tea are arranged. Photographer Rashid Lombard wants us to pose as a family but Ruschka is suddenly more interested in the refreshments. I cut her a slice of chocolate cake covered with layers of cream and chocolate flake. I take her onto my lap and she licks the cream and chocolate from her fingers. For the first time, the three of us are together, surrounded by scores of friendly people.

I steady her plate with one hand and place my other hand on my husband's knee. Ruschka holds her plate with her left hand and stuffs a piece of cake into her mouth with her right, all the while grinning, her eyes sparkling. Rashid clicks his shutter and captures that single moment in our lives when the three of us blended into one whole, merged by an unequalled feeling of joyousness which is written on our faces for all the world to see.

CHAPTER TEN

Ruschka is wearing a white track-top with a blue hood. I am in the back of the car keeping her amused while her father drives. We are on the N2, the national road leading to the scenic Garden Route approaching the Gordon's Bay turn-off. At the intersection, police are blockading the road, stopping every car. They look into ours and ask where we are going. To the shops in Gordon's Bay because our child is restless. They peer at us closely, decide that we are genuine and let us through. We wind our way down the long road to the seaside, drive past the shops at Gordon's Bay and head towards the next beach at the Strand. When we get there, we see hundreds of people converging on the beach from all sides. Local Strand residents, young and old join those who have managed to slip through the police cordons like us. Coinciding with the sixth anniversary of the launch of the UDF, we are protesting against segregated beaches.

Most of the Cape beaches are sign-posted "Whites Only" and today we are going to ignore the signs. The original plan was to all gather here at the Strand but with the heavy police presence, people are making their way to the beaches nearest them. I hear later that while we were at the Strand, others were at Blouberg and Muizenberg.

The colourful crowds, most dressed in warmish clothes on this sunny winter's day, are spread all along the pavement bordering the beach. Here and there, somebody hoists up a poster: "Beaches are God-given, they belong to all."

Protecting the sea from the people is a row of policemen standing all along the water's edge, reining in barking dogs on long leashes. It is a sight I will never forget for as long as I live.

I try to find a safe spot for Ruschka and myself in case of trouble. On the left-hand side of the crowd there is a low jetty jutting into the sea where anglers usually cast their fishing lines. Today the jetty is deserted. I take Ruschka's hand and make my way to the edge so that we can watch the waves lapping against its side. To distract her, I tell her we are going to see if we can spot the fish in the water below. We lie flat on our stomachs, gazing down into the frothy dull blue water. I am so happy that I am here with my husband not far away and my child next to me. And I am so proud of the organisation we have built.

I remember how we ran around six years ago to set up the secret meetings to discuss the formation of the UDF. Eight local leaders had met secretly. They were Zoli Malindi, Oscar Mphetha, Virginia Engel, Christmas Tinto, Mildred Ramakaba-Lesiea, Cheryl Carolus, Trevor Manuel and Johnny Issel. They decided that for this to work, we needed broad participation in the decision to form the organisation. I was working at the Churches Urban Planning Commission and we helped to organise five consultative meetings bringing together over a hundred activists identified through our contacts at *Grassroots* newspaper. We brought them together at five different homes simultaneously and secretly, to spend a full day studying the implications of the government's plan to give a qualified vote to Coloured and Indian people and excluding Africans.

At each meeting, activists made lists of which organisations and individuals were to be invited to form the core of the UDF. We had mobilised thousands upon thousands not by magic but by organisation and through the effort of hundreds of these dedicated young people.

Ruschka has become aware that my mind is not with her and is tired of the game I pretend to be playing. She is tugging at me to take her onto the beach so that she can go into the water. She is a child who makes a beeline for the sea whenever we visit. Johnny, all his children and myself had this one thing in common. We all loved the water and took to it like fishes. In the summer months, swimming was our main recreational activity.

We are expecting Archbishop Tutu to arrive to head the protest but he has in the meantime been advised to make a detour to Bloubergstrand, a beach on the West Coast to which protestors are being redirected. Ruschka keeps on tugging and demands to know why she cannot go in the water.

"Those men with the dogs don't want us to go into the water, Ruschka."

"Why, mummy, why?"

I don't know what to say. I suddenly realise that this child has no idea of race. I have never introduced her to the concept and how do I now explain to her that she cannot go into the water because this is a white beach and that she is not white. I do not want to do it. For so long our central passion has been building a non-racial society where all of us can just be human beings, not punished for the colour of our skin.

She is insisting. What should I say?

I swallow hard. "Well, Ruschka, you can't go in the water because you are not white."

For a moment she is still, as if she is pondering what I have said. I am relieved that the tugging has stopped. Then she looks down at her white track-top and grips it with two fingers, pulling it away from her body. "But, mommy, I am white."

My heart sinks down into my stomach, through my buttocks, through the plank structure of the jetty and plops into the swirling waves below. I am flooded with a feeling of shame unlike any I have felt before. This child truly has no idea of race and I have the task of teaching her its meaning in our world. I am about to become an instrument of this evil system bringing a man-made division into my daughter's undivided mind.

"They say our skin has to be white for us to be white. If our skin is not white, then we cannot swim on most of the beaches in Cape Town. But this is not what Allah says. Allah says we are all the same. This is what this bad government is saying and we are trying to change it."

The religious interpretation is supported by the Freedom Charter that guides our movement: "We, the people of South Africa, declare for all our country and the world to know that South Africa belongs to all who live in it, black and white, and that no government can justly claim authority unless it is based on the will of all the people . . ."

I hear the screech of police vans pulling up in the distance and see the men jumping out brandishing batons and quirts. The crowd runs in all directions with police giving chase. I lift Ruschka into my arms and trot as fast as I can, trying to reach the car. The policemen with the dogs leave the edge of the water and run after the protestors, some of whom get bitten and are rushed to the mobile first-aid van set up by the UDF.

We reach the car just as I see her father come running along from a different direction. As he unlocks the door, we hear the loud thud of gunshots and hear the screams as people try to get away. Later we hear that some were not so lucky and landed in hospital with birdshot wounds peppered on their backs.

Over the next months, nothing can stop the tide. In the midst of it all, family duties are the first to be sacrificed.

The phone rings. Who could it be? It's nearly ten at night. I hear my sister's voice. "I just thought I would call you because today is Junaid's birthday and you have not called him yet to wish him."

I am so embarrassed. I am never good at remembering birthdays but Junaid's I have a special penchant for neglecting. Every year when it comes to late evening, my sister calls, embarrassed too that I have once again for-gotten.

"Oh my God, where is he? Can I speak with him? I am sorry. I don't know why I keep forgetting." I mumble on incoherently.

My sister is gracious as always. "It's fine but when you did not call, I thought I better remind you."

Why do I keep on forgetting Junaid's birthday?

CHAPTER ELEVEN

A thin mist forms over my eyeballs. I blink and blink again. It is not the bright morning sunlight filtering through the trees next to St. George's Cathedral that threatens to blind me but a deep emotion welling up in my chest, into my throat, reaching my eyes. Through the mist I stare at the white schoolchildren dressed in expensive blazers and boater hats. The banks of the protest river have widened, collecting them in the steady endless flow. Their boaters bob up and down amongst the banners stretching across the crowd.

Not a single policeman or armoured vehicle is in sight. A few weeks ago, we were surrounded when we attempted to march in Burg Street, around the corner from this spot.

As if the schoolchildren have triggered something, my heart starts thumping and I am back in that day, dark and cloudy.

The idea is to deliver a memorandum to parliament to protest against police violence. Weeks ago, my mother and other United Women's Congress women marched, were arrested and brought to court at a special night sitting. Following the women's example, ninety-seven academics donned their academic gowns, filed into the city centre and were arrested. In desperation, church workers and priests knelt down in protest in the road in front of security headquarters in Loop Street and were mercilessly beaten. When Tutu, Jakes and other leading educationists hastily convened a march in protest against these beatings they too were arrested.

We are a hotchpotch of community protestors assembling in Burg Street like a wave rolling towards the police. Eight of us, arms hooked together, occupy the front row of the march. We line up across the road in front of the church as others fall into formation behind us. We do not know what to expect. The police in their dull-blue uniforms are prepared for a standoff. But then so are we. They have brought a new gadget with them. Something that looks like a concrete-mixing machine with a long nozzle. I look up at it and think dear God, will I see my child today? What is this thing going to shoot into us? Will I die? I'd rather die than get seriously hurt.

We confer quickly and decide to sit down in the street as agreed earlier in the church hall. The crowd takes its cue from us and slowly the mass of bodies sag onto the ground. Across the street in front of us are a long row of police armed with guns. I see no quirts or batons. The next thing, a purple liquid sprouts from this gadget, spraying onto the protestors. Everybody runs in different directions not knowing what it is. My coat and scarf are coloured with streaks of purple as I run towards Greenmarket Square. Then I hear a roar rising from the crowd. I turn and see a young man sitting on the nozzle of this new police gadget. He has clambered up onto the machine from the crowd and taken control of the nozzle, directing it onto the walls of the adjacent buildings. As the purple dye pours out in a torrent splashing onto the walls, fear turns to laughter. I cannot stop laughing as the lone protestor turns the oppressive atmosphere into a carnival-like celebration.

The police recover from the shock of our laughter and we run as they retaliate with batons and teargas. I stumble and choke as the gas overwhelms me. People are collapsing in the street around me. As the marchers flee in different directions, their eyes are streaming, as are mine. I dash blindly down the road, removing my coat and scarf, rolling them up to conceal the incriminating purple stains from the dull-blue men bounding up behind me.

Today there is not a policeman in sight and Capetonians of all persuasions pour into line behind their leaders. At the head of the procession is the Archbishop Tutu in his cerise clerical garb with a silver cross hanging around his neck. To his left is the mayor of Cape Town, Gordon Oliver, dressed in a charcoal suit and a red tie and next to him is Alan Boesak with a red-and-black clerical gown resembling an academic gown. To his right is Sheikh Nazeem Mohammed, wearing a traditional black prayer robe with a white starched skull cap perched on his head. Next to him is Jakes Gerwel in his favourite grey-blue suit, blue shirt and UWC tie and next to him is Jay Naidoo, Cosatu general secretary, in his dark pants and blue sweater underneath a dark blazer. I find it fascinating that as protests become more prominent, so do the male leaders. Not to suggest that they were not around when the hard work had to be done but they shared the hard work equally with the women during the darkest days. In many instances, the burden fell more heavily on the women as they often could move around more freely and were less easily detected by the police.

One arm hooked into another, then into another, the leaders form a united barrier, as if they are able to protect the teeming crowds surging up behind them.

As the mass of people moves slowly down Adderley Street, I jump onto a side wall to have a better view. I have been covering protests and then organising protests for nearly ten years and have never seen such a crowd in Cape Town. The closest I can remember was the funeral of Imām Abdullah Haron in 1969. I was eleven years old when my father called my mother from a shop near Salt River.

"Raymie, bring the children through," my father said. "If you come to the side of Groote Schuur Hospital, you will be able to see the funeral. You must bring them."

We stood on the hospital premises that bordered the Muslim cemetery. In the distance, I saw thousands upon thousands of men winding their way behind a funeral bier bearing the imām's body. My father was somewhere in that crowd. They had walked about twenty kilometres from City Park stadium in Athlone where the funeral was held, to the cemetery in Salt River. By choosing to walk that distance, they had found the only legitimate way they could to voice their outrage. Nobody knew the detail of his death. All we knew was that he had died after being in police detention for 133 days and that his body was covered in multiple bruises, twenty-eight in all. The authorities said that he had accidentally fallen down a flight of stairs.

I will never forget the day he was buried because it was my sister's birthday – 29 September 1969. I was acutely aware of how upset everybody around me was. My father had come home and was trying his best to persuade the Vigilance Association committee not to go ahead with a fundraising film to be held at the hall that night.

"We cannot show a movie on the night that the imām has been buried," said my dad. But he failed to have his way. At about 8.30 p.m. that evening, I was splashing water over my feet before going to bed when I felt the house shaking. At first I thought it was a big truck passing by on Ottery Road. We lived on a main road and were used to the heavy traffic and noise. But then I heard my dad shouting that we had to get out of the house. I dashed barefoot through the front door and on to the pavement. The earth was shaking and we did not know what to do. Would it open up and swallow us? After a while, when the earth's shaking subsided and we felt less unsteady on our feet, we went back into the house.

That night I could not sleep. And it was worse when I heard the phone ringing in the middle of the night. Somebody had called to say there would be another tremor and it would be best for us to be outside our homes. My mom had earlier told us all to put our slippers and gowns ready so that we could just grab them and run. But now I heard my parents speaking in hushed tones and my father saying that he was not going to take the family outside into the cold. "We trust in Allah that we will be safe," he said.

Like many others, he believed that the earth shook that night because it had to receive the imām's body and that God was showing his anger at this great injustice.

That was the last time I had seen so huge a crowd and our hearts were heavy with grief.

Today there is a lightness in the air, a sense of unity that brings a certain calm to the crowd and the absence of the security forces helps to reinforce the idea that peace is possible. Part of the crowd is able to flow into the City Hall. The rest wait patiently on the parade opposite for the leaders to appear on the balcony.

An ANC flag is draped across the balcony of the City Hall. For the first time, leaders have access to the balcony. Tutu and Boesak hold loud-hailers in their hands as they address the crowds. A city hall is supposed to be a place that is accessible to all citizens. But in our city, it belongs to the white community.

Seeing Jakes, Tutu and others up on that balcony makes my eyes misty again. Oh dear, today is going to be one of those weepy days. One of those days when I am not sure that I am really seeing what I am seeing. I have become so accustomed to the absence of peace, to the police brutality, to the constant violence in our lives, that my body is primed for that. I expect and brace myself at all times for attack. But here I am merging in a sea of humanity for the first time completely convinced that it cannot be long before we can enjoy some peace. If I had only known, I could have told Mozena to bring Ruschka through to the city center so that she could be part of this crowd. But this morning I had no idea what the day would bring.

As I look around me, I cannot help thinking what a disaster it could have been if De Klerk had not instructed the police to back off. Their absence helped enormously to reduce the tension that has been tearing this city apart. With P W Botha finally dislodged, De Klerk has the sense to realise that the multitudes are overtaking him and his party.

I arrange the pictures across my desk and decide which ones will go on the front page. I choose four. Three of the big march and one of the campus protests where students march with an array of posters. "Education not intimidation". "Education not detention".

I draw the outline of the front page design for the printer, Shaheed, who will feed the detail into the computer. All front-page pictures will be in full colour. Pictures inside of the campus action and academic protests in the city are in black and white. I pencil in the headline: "On the March". It's all so easy. I suddenly think of those days when we first tried our hands at more-or-less irregular community newspapers. We used to have to make lettraset headlines, rubbing each letter on to the page. Then came the bits of text that had been separately typeset. This had to be pasted onto the page, leaving space for photographs and captions which we cropped with a special knife.

Producing *Grassroots*, our first regular community newspaper, was slightly more sophisticated with headlines being set by the typesetter. The end product was still pages with bits of paper stuck all over it that had to be physically transported to the printers.

Mike Norton, a veteran journalist who worked full-time for *Grassroots*, one day placed all the pages on the roof of his car to free his hands so that he could unlock the car door. Then he got in, forgetting to take the pages with him. The next thing he saw them slip down the windscreen, scattering onto the cobble-paved streets. Mike found himself running up and down trying to pick up pages and little bits of text and pictures that had come undone. The Cape wind proved a greater irritation than the security police that day as bits of paper twirled out of reach.

Now, as I save all stories onto a disc that I will slip into a big white envelope with the sketch of the lay-out design of the pages, my mind rambles on in the direction that the business of making up today's paper has prompted.

My thoughts go to the days when none of us owned computers and few owned cars. I smile as I think of Trevor Manuel on his motorbike. At least he has a second-hand car now, getting him from place to place. When my father bought me a second-hand red Golf in 1981, he was one of the comrades who chided me. I was too embarrassed to be seen in this car because it looked too bright and sparkling, even though it was a used car.

"You are not going to be able to go anywhere in that car," said Trevor. It just did not fit into our notion of living a life close to the poor. I was about twenty-three years old then. My eldest brother, Joe, was happy to accept my dad's gift of a red Golf after I confessed that I would have difficulty in being seen with such an obviously rich-looking vehicle.

I once tried to ride Trevor's bike myself, moving it slowly out of my mother's yard and into the back street. The bike was big and heavy and as I came out of the yard, I tried to turn right into the street, only to discover that I was not skilled enough or strong enough to turn it. Instead of going right, I went straight towards the neighbour's wall across the road. The bike and I tipped over, bringing any further ambition to ride to an abrupt end. This was definitely not for me. I had to grudgingly accept my limitations. I knew my parents did not mind me experimenting but would not at all approve of my riding a motorbike. For years they had been reluctant to buy me a bicycle and said I could buy one once I left school and earned my own money. It was one of the first things I did.

I love cycling and until I had my own I used to steal a ride from whoever had a bike in the neighbourhood. Sheikh Nazeem saw me one day and the next day, he spoke to our class in madressa.

"Young girls can hurt themselves on bicycles," he said, looking straight at me.

The problem for me was that he was my religious teacher and lived in our back street. There was very little I could do that he would not know about. We used to love playing soccer in the street – boys and girls all together. This was acceptable when we were young children but when a girl became a young lady, when she had her period, she was expected not to play soccer in the back street. It was all very frustrating.

Sheikh somehow represented an extension of my dad but we had often tussled over the years. He wanted us to wear tightly pinned scarves covering our foreheads and all our hair. I was quite happy with a scarf tied under my chin with my front hair peeping out and I told him so. Once he gave us a long lecture about girls walking down Park Road with boys after school in the afternoon. Up went my hand and I confessed to the madressa class.

"Sheikh is talking about me," I said. "These boys are in my class. We sit at the same desks the whole day, then we walk down to the station at Steurhof. We ride to Wittebome and then walk down Park Road. Am I supposed to pretend I don't know them when I walk down Park Road?"

He used to shake his head when I asked these questions in the class. I could challenge him and often demand explanations because of the fondness that existed between us.

As I work on the layout of the newspaper I gaze at the photograph numbered four and feel a sense of great pride to see him walking next to Archbishop Tutu. He looks so smart in his black clerical dress, gold-rimmed sunglasses and greying beard. I am aware that he has offended many in the community by poor judgements that have led to splits. But he is too enmeshed in my life, I am too closely tied with his good side to be completely put off by his bad side.

There was a time when I despaired of the Muslim community, making me reject the religion. To see Sheikh alongside the other non-Muslim leaders walking at the head of the pulsating crowd reminds me of a night long long ago. I was sitting on the prayer mat with my dad. We had just finished the evening prayers and I needed to speak with him. His face had turned grey as I spoke.

"Dad, I don't think I can believe in this religion that does nothing in the face of injustice," I had said. "I don't see what use it has in my life when those who implement it ignore all the major injunctions of the Qur'ān."

My father had struggled to speak. He had tried to explain to me his obsession with education. He wanted us to be educated so that we could fulfil an important message of Islam and that was to seek to acquire knowledge and broaden the mind. But the religious community had warned that once people get educated they turned against the religion. He had argued that this was not necessarily the case and now I was coming to him proving them right. I had seen his pain but had had to be true to my own feelings.

"Dad, the discussion here is about whether we can eat cheese or not. For me, this is truly ridiculous. The prophet made the halaal laws so that we should not eat anything that is unhygienic and unhealthy. At the time, people used to eat dead carcasses they found abandoned and the prophet had to stop this practice. I cannot see why we are fighting about the cheese which may have a drop of animal fat in it when people are starving and oppressed in our country."

"Think about what you are saying," my dad had said.

"I have been thinking about it all the time," I had replied. "We are choosing to make a big fuss over nothing and no fuss over big issues. Where are our imāms and our sheikhs? They want to stay in their separate little groups and not reach out to other South Africans."

My dad had got up from the prayer mat, folded it and placed it on the bed. "You are right but it does not mean you should reject the religion. You should work towards changing the levels of education and things will change slowly over time."

I am so glad that my dad has lived to see the change. I cannot see him in any of the pictures of the crowds marching through town but I know he is somewhere there. Perhaps I can spot his red fez. I keep on looking through the smiling sea of faces but cannot see the distinctive hat. My rejection of the rituals of Islam had ended two years later in 1980, when the faint sound of my dad's voice had pierced the room where I was being detained. They were about to drive me to Port Elizabeth and had allowed my parents to deliver some clean clothing. What could I do to attract them? How could I let them know that I was alive and strong? What would carry my voice as far as it could go?

I had taken a deep breath: "Ya Nabee salaam a'leika. Ya Rasool salaam, a'leika . . ."(Oh prophet, peace be upon you. Oh prophet, peace be upon you.)

It was a hymn-like song I had learnt as a child that carried my voice down the long corridor.

"Beida!" my dad had responded before the cops hurriedly ordered them to leave.

Angrily, a cop had barged into the room, telling me that I was breaking the law. I had stopped, satisfied that I had made contact with my parents. The incident forced me to acknowledge how integral this religion, warts and all, was to my life.

I gather all the photographs together, numbering the ones that will be used in the last edition for the year. I want to leave UWC at the end of this year so that I can sort out my family life for a few weeks. My step-daughter, Leila, is living with us now and her brother, Yasser, will soon be coming to stay as well. They are at high school and need help with homework and teenage problems. We have rented a house in Fairways and live together as a family for the first time. I feel intensely tired. My muscles are aching and my head feels tight.

After seeing those white schoolchildren merge into the teeming mass of humanity this week, it seems so possible that political activity may normalise and if it does, I need to assess what I want to do with my life. Perhaps I will at last have time to learn how to bake a chocolate cake.

CHAPTER TWELVE

I take Ruschka from her father's shoulders and hoist her onto mine. The sun is beating down onto us. She has a white sun hat on her little head. Her dad goes in search of water or a cool drink but finds that all the kiosks on the parade and surrounding shops are sold out. All around us heads bob up and down, peering, jostling in the hope of securing the best vantage point. The constant movement at the edges of the crowd indicate that more people are joining us by the minute, quickening the racing pulse of the crowd. It is close to 3 p.m. on 11 February 1990. We have been standing on the parade since 1 p.m. On all sides, the marshals with their red head-bands are trying their best to keep the crowds inside the cordoned-off areas. Everybody wants to be as close to the City Hall as possible so that they can catch a glimpse of the man who is about to be released from prison after twenty-seven years. It is the moment we have been waiting for. The moment we will see Nelson Mandela.

This morning it came as a great shock when we looked at the Sunday papers and saw a smiling tall man, immaculate in a grey suit towering above F W de Klerk. Nothing could have prepared me for that regal image – slender, youthful, light, yet gloriously aged. When the news first filtered through to us that he had started quiet negotiations with the authorities, there was a lot of scepticism amongst activists. There were some who suggested that he was making a deal and would sell us out. There were others who felt that he was old and out of touch and would have no idea of the sentiments of people on the ground. Instead of being excited today, I am apprehensive. I am not worried so much that he was making strange deals but worried because I feel we are in disarray. As the afternoon goes by, I am more and more gripped by the feeling of unease. Mandela is not arriving and the crowd is growing restless. By 5 p.m. he is still not there and I hear shooting in the distance. The crowd lurches forward.

Oh my God. Why are they shooting?

What if they shoot Mandela?

Who are they shooting?

There are people looting shops, says somebody in the crowd. There are gangsters taking over on the fringes.

Minutes later my friend, Shireen Misbach, clambers onto the wall of the post office so that she can position herself to have a good view of the City Hall balcony where Mandela will make his appearance. A bullet comes flying past her head, sending her scurrying down from her vantage point. "There is some kind of shoot-out," she says.

"We are going to be killed today." Police are shooting at youthful gangsters.

"Why don't they just arrest them?"

A feeling of panic arises in my stomach. Blood rushes to my face. Small fat ladybirds of sweat crawl down my forehead into my eyebrows. I am hot and suddenly very scared. In times of crisis, I seldom panic, but today I cannot control my sense of anxiety. A sense of over-protectiveness overwhelms me, enveloping me unexpectedly like a tornado, sweeping me away with my child. I am moving away from family and friends, leaving them behind. Moving away from the crowd, trying to reach safety. Through the crowds, into District Six and into our parked car.

Ruschka is quiet and not her usual demanding self. Blown from the crowd, away from the sound of bullets, the storm encasing me subsides. My heartbeat slows down as I hold my child close to me. It is cooler in the car and this reduces the anxiety but not the worry. I had always expected this day to be a very happy day. Now that it has come, worry grips me like an iron vice.

They had sprung Mandela's release on us the day before, forcing everybody to abandon everything and rush to UWC for a meeting. The announcement of the release had come about 4 p.m. on Saturday afternoon. It had come a week after De Klerk had committed his government to negotiations and had unbanned the relevant organisations.

Sitting in the car, I know that we are in disarray. Most of our organisations have been smashed. Comrades are recovering from years of detention. In the past few months, Trevor has been released from detention after three years, Johnny, Cheryl and Mildred Lesea have come out of hiding and Oscar has been released from prison. There is in-fighting amongst them.

Most of us are just emotionally drained and tired. I am so worried that Mandela is coming into a situation where we are not able to provide the proper organisational support. It is showing so strongly today. We are not running a tight organisational ship and have been charging around trying to contain a situation that is increasingly dangerous.

We seem not to have put enough marshals in place, nor an effective communication system to liaise properly with those leaving the prison in Paarl and the rest of us here in the city. Our lack of control is making it easier for the police to justify shooting the small group of criminals taking their chances.

I calm my nerves and go back to the parade as the afternoon shifts into early evening. The sun is beginning to set when the black Mercedez Benz carrying Mandela slides slowly through the crowds in front of the City Hall. Through the chaos, he somehow is led into the building and then onto the balcony. In the flurry, he does not have his reading glasses with him and one of the comrades offers him his own. I see his face hazily in the dusk.

"Friends, comrades and fellow South Africans. I greet you all in the name of peace, democracy and freedom for all."

The wave of excitement washing through the crowd pierces my armour as cheers punctuate his speech.

"I send special greetings to the people of Cape Town, this city which has been my home for three decades. Your mass marches and other forms of struggle have served as a constant source of strength to all political prisoners."

It's hard to guage the size of the crowd. The estimates during the course of the afternoon fall between 150 000 and 250 000. The earlier panic has subsided and in between the cheers, there is a hushed silence. He changes briefly to Xhosa, his mother-tongue:

"Maqabane! (Comrades.)

"Andinawo amazwi obuciko endinokuwathetha namhlanje ngaphandle kokuthi ubomi bam obuzayo busezandleni zenu." (I do not have eloquent words to speak today except to say that my life in the future is in your hands.)

Pride passes in waves from one body to another pressed tightly together as we strain to see his every gesture.

"The destruction caused by apartheid on our subcontinent is incalculable. The fabric of family life of millions of my people has been shattered. Millions are homeless and unemployed. Our economy lies in ruins and our people are embroiled in political strife."

I hold Ruschka close to me as he speaks. She is too young to understand but perhaps she will remember this day.

"Our resort to the armed struggle in 1960 with the formation of the military wing of the ANC, Umkhonto we Sizwe, was a purely defensive action against the violence of apartheid. The factors that necessitated the armed struggle still exist today. We have no option but to continue. We express the hope that a climate conducive to a negotiated settlement will be created soon so that there may no longer be the need for the armed struggle."

I sigh with relief and know that many activists on the parade are exhaling. He has not sold out. He has not come to any deals with the state behind our backs. His speech is warm, congratulatory, yet also placing us all on full alert.

I kiss Ruschka on both cheeks, on her eyelids, on her nose, hugging her as his rich voice concludes with his famous 1964 statement from the dock that shudders through his large frame.

"I have fought against white domination and I have fought against black domination. I have cherished the ideal of a democratic and free society in which all persons live together in harmony and with equal opportunities. It is an ideal which I hope to live for and to achieve. But if needs be, it is an ideal for which I am prepared to die."

CHAPTER THIRTEEN

"Write me a story about witches, mummy," says Ruschka. "Don't tell me about what happened to you and daddy. It makes me too sad."

She is five years old but has just reminded me that she and all our children deserve a carefree childhood. A childhood of witches, of Peter Pan and Molo Songololo. Without the violence that has scarred our generation. She can be real babyish at times so when she says something like this, I look at her more closely, unsure if she is maturing too fast.

Her gaze is steady and momentarily I see the dark pupils of an old woman. It never ceases to amaze me how a small child is a combination of young and old energies that are suddenly visible when the alternation comes abruptly.

I fill the kettle with water, plug it into the socket and open the cupboard to find a cup and saucer. I cannot drink tea from a mug. I prefer a thin-rimmed cup because it somehow enhances the taste.

"I can't believe it, mummy, I did it. This is the story of two kittens." She pushes the pages into my hands. There are five pages of drawings stapled together, a product of her day at pre-school. She asks me to write words onto each page to express the story she has sketched.

I start the story as depicted: "Two kittens went to a race track one day. They saw the starter shoot his gun. They watched the bums and backs of the runners . . ."

For once the telephone is ignored as it rings in the sunny room where I sit and write all day. The expected call about the ongoing taxi violence in the Western Cape will have to wait for another time. The story of the two kittens needs attention. We kneel on the floor beside the bed, the two of us sharing a cup of tea, and decide on the words appropriate to each sketch . . . "The one kitten belonged to a little girl. Her mummy was wearing earrings and bangles. Both kittens ran to the winner of the race."

Delighted with her story, she rushes off to show her work to the neighbour, Denise, who lives behind our house. I laugh, thanking God for giving her to me as a happy warm glow glides through my body. She has brought a certain balance into my life that has made it easy to leave behind the pressured life of activist and organiser.

Once the negotiations had started with a formidable team of local and exiled leaders, I had felt free to go back to my writing. At first I had been unsure, and had joined the local branch of the ANC but after six months, I had known this was not for me and had resigned. If I was to go back to my career as a journalist, I believed it would not be compatible with party membership.

I wait for her return in the lane outside our kitchen door as the sun beats down on my flushed cheeks, burning away the dark images of the past decade.

After years of rush, it is pleasant to work from home, to be able to help the children with their homework and to see Ruschka's happy little face in the afternoons when she comes home from school. I have been learning to bake a chocolate cake, allowing Ruschka and her friend Waldo to lick the left-over batter from the bowl.

"Mix us a whole bowl one day, mom," says Ruschka. "We want to lick all of it." I smile, unsure whether I can or should oblige.

I must settle down to some work. There has just been so much excitement with exiles coming home and prisoners being released that it's not always easy to keep up with my writing. The one thing I did not like about my job at UWC was the long drive to Bellville in the morning. Working from home saves time. But I had also always enjoyed getting onto the train in Wynberg and travelling to the city centre, no heavy traffic and no hassle with having to find parking. If our train system were more extensive, I would really not bother having a car. Come to think of it, it was the journeying from high school and back every day that helped develop my love for the train.

I would get on at Wittebome station in the morning, ride three stations to Steurhof, get off and walk for about fifteen minutes up a long road to South Peninsula High School. The most unpleasant part of travelling by train was having to check whether the coach was for whites or non-whites. But this did not detract from my love for train travel itself. When I left home to study journalism in Grahamstown, I travelled by train. My family and friends were all standing on the platform at Cape Town station as the train slowly pulled out of the station. My dad had cried all over me as I said goodbye and this was a big embarrassment for a nineteen-year-old. Imagine her father holding her and crying in front of all her friends. One would expect mothers to do this but not fathers. As the train moved further away, I saw my family and friends grow smaller and smaller as they continued to wave. I looked up at Table Mountain, watching it recede into the distance and wept.

My dad was really the softy in the family. He spanked me only once in my life and then we both cried. My mom was the one who did not hesitate to threaten the cane, although I can only remember her whacking my brother Mansoor and I once when we came home from the library arguing, the one complaining about the other.

"I don't want to hear stories from either of you," she said. "I don't know who to believe." Whack, whack. "This must stop. Just sort out your problems."

There was no arguing with my mother. We used to call her "sergeant major". My father was the one who was always calling round-table family discussions. This irritated my mother, who preferred laying down the law and seeing to it that we all obeyed.

Now that I have a child of my own, I appreciate the different strengths they had brought to the parenting process. Our parents are our first role models and I had the benefit of choosing a little of each approach to develop a style that I considered suited my children. Leila was nearly sixteen and going through teenage difficulties. Yasser was a quiet child and was with us temporarily and would be going back to his mother soon. I do not have a cane for Ruschka but I have hung a belt at the back of the kitchen door.

"Now where is that belt?

"Where is it?

"Let me fetch that belt," I say when she does not want to get into bed. She scampers down the passage as fast as her little legs can carry her and jumps into her bed. The belt has not come off that hook in the kitchen but I am leaving it there just in case it is needed.

I work for Africa Information Afrique (AIA), a Canadian news agency with offices in Harare. After the unbanning of the ANC in February, my personal future had been unsure. But the uncertainty was brief. I had very quickly realised that all I wanted to do was go back to my life as a journalist. With the political process in safe hands, the negotiations slowly getting under way, the time had come to take up where I had left off ten years earlier. I had always felt that circumstances beyond my control had wrenched me from my position at the *Cape Times* and taken me on the roller coaster ride of resistance to apartheid.

It is a thrill once again to see my copy in print in the local newspaper *South*, a member user of AIA, and other alternative newspapers in the country. It is good for my confidence to hear that newspapers in eleven Southern African countries as well as in Canada are member users and are placing my stories.

It's not been easy making the shift from active participant to observer of a process. My problem is that I fluctuate between feeling normal and writing easily to being overwhelmed by emotion and unable to write. Although the feelings have been buried deeply, they are so easily evoked by a word or a comment or a scene. Entering a courtroom to cover a story one day I find my heart thumping against my chest. The floor beneath my feet feels unsteady. I leave as soon as I can, unsure why I suddenly feel sick but learning fast what triggers memories of the dentist's chair.

The day after the courtroom episode, I set out to meet veteran ANC lawyer and returned exile, Albie Sachs.

All around us, people are dying. They are mysteriously being flung out of trains in Johannesburg. Masked men are bursting into homes and mowing down entire families.

I want our negotiators to find the killers and the torturers. I want them to put P W Botha, F W de Klerk and all their generals on trial.

I don't want to see Mostert or Spyker van Wyk on the street – they are nails lodged deep in my tender flesh. I don't think I would be able to bear it. I would like somebody to hit them for me, to hurt them like they hurt so many of us. How can our negotiators be talking about amnesty for these men? We need trials. Even if we cannot try all of them, we should try some of them.

I explain this to Albie. As we talk, I try not to focus on his arm. The stump hangs loosely at the side of his body, covered by his rolled-up jersey sleeve. I am used to seeing dead comrades but sitting in front of me was one who had survived a car-bomb attack. He lived to tell the story, unlike dearest Ashley. And he is saying something that is hard for me to grasp.

"Punishing these people will keep the cycle of retribution and counter-retribution going on and on," he says.

"We need to break that cycle. Only our generation can do it if we have the courage to face the past with honesty but without vindictiveness."

"But these people cannot just get away with all the damage they have done!" I expostulate.

"They won't get away with it. Everybody will know what he or she did and they will have to live with that," he says. "Prosecuting a few of them won't make a difference. But successfully changing this system of racial discrimination that they believe in will mean complete defeat. That will give me greater pleasure than seeing a few people suffer," he says.

I feel confused. He is challenging all my assumptions. Still, what he says does connect with something deep inside of me. I want to find a way to move on. To wipe away the images of those groups of white men surrounding me, interrogating me, hitting me. But how am I going to do that when all around me I see people dying and I believe these same men to be responsible for the mayhem? I cannot do it. Albie is not the only one who is speaking this new language. I begin to think more carefully about what Nelson Mandela and one of our key military leaders, Joe Slovo, are saying.

Mandela was Commander-in-Chief of the military wing of the ANC. He had advocated armed action against the enemy and we had supported his call. Although I am not one of the many activists who received military training, I am close to those comrades who were part of the underground structures and had assisted them with raising money, setting up communications and supplying help with various personal needs.

I admire them for their willingness to physically fight against an apparatus that appeared all-powerful, that was destroying our lives with violence.

I remember how clearly Archbishop Tutu expressed our feelings in 1987 when he said: "The church regards all types of violence as evil; but if one faces two evils one must ask: what is the lesser evil? The most dramatic example was the evil of Nazism on the one hand and the evil of going to war, on the other.

"The best option was going to war in order to put an end to gas chambers and concentration camps. I, Desmond Tutu, must say that I, for my part, think that we have reached that point in South Africa. If the international community lets us down in terms of pressure that could lead to change, and if the white population remains as it is – then we have no other choice."

Now we are being called upon to desist from fighting and to consider how we are going to live with those whom we consider to be our enemy.

"Something has to be done about these people," I say to Albie. "Look at De Klerk. Did you see how jaunty and happy he was in the months after he released Mandela? The man was so sure of himself. And you know why?"

"Why?" says Albie as he pulls on his sunhat.

"Well ..."

"Before you explain, let's walk down to the beach," he says.

He is staying with his friend Dusty on Clifton beach. We make our way down the steps onto the soft white sands and walk towards the distant boulders at the far end of the beach.

The water glistens in the late afternoon winter sun. Two gulls sweep low down across the waves, their wings extending as they glide gracefully, close to the surface, ready to plunge into the water for their evening meal.

"De Klerk knew exactly what he was doing when he released Mandela," I say. "Our organisations were smashed. He felt he had control over the situation. His party has used the five years from 1985 to try and bring the movement to its knees. You could argue that they did not succeed. But my sense is that in the short term they did. They destroyed people, weakened them, killed many and then brought Mandela into this weakened situation. Knowing this, they are in a good position to force you guys to compromise at Codesa."

Albie is a member of the ANC's constitutional and legal department and is intimately involved in the negotiations process being driven by the Congress for a Democratic South Africa, popularly known as Codesa. I am able to give him a sense of the feelings of people on the ground and he gives me insights into the drama at Kempton Park, where the negotiations are proceeding.

"My first prize would be putting De Klerk and others on trial," I say.

"That's not going to work," he says.

I am taken aback when he changes the subject and offers me a job as a part-time research assistant. As I listen to him, I know that this will be an opportunity of a lifetime, to work with somebody so intimately involved in the negotiations and to gather information helpful to that process.

We reach the end of the beach and he touches the large boulder that towers above us.

"This is a ritual I remember as a child," he says. It is as if he is paying homage to the eternity of the rock representing continuity in his life. He grew up on Clifton beach and when he returned after so many years in exile he had found somebody who could offer him a room to help him reconnect with his past.

"Mom, please bring me a Barbie doll." Ruschka tugs at my jacket sleeve. "I want a Barbie doll, mom." I am saying goodbye to my parents at the airport on my way to Holland.

"I'll see, Ruschka." I am not keen to put the purchase of a Barbie doll on my to-do list. For years now I have been resisting this demand. I am not going to easily find an excuse now that she is six years old. And I am feeling quite guilty. My personal life is in a shambles. A month ago, holding a small suitcase in one hand and Ruschka by the other, I had left our Fairways home and moved back to my parents. Ruschka was bewildered then and is bewildered now. I find it hard to explain to her why I have left her father. In fact I am not able to explain this to anyone. My dearest and only sister, trained as a medical doctor, has some idea but generally I prefer to keep quiet and deal with this very difficult matter on my own. I am not sure whether it's a question of pride or fear or the need to be private but I cannot speak about what I consider to be an intimate union with another. I have given this man my heart and soul and he holds it in his possession. I have physically torn myself away from him but I cannot speak because emotionally I am still with him. How can it be any other way? He is the only one that I could truly relate to after my detention and torture. He has gone through the same traumas and is similarly obsessed with destroying a system that has brought us so much grief.

How does one explain to a small child the intricacies of adult emotional relations?

I am on my way to Holland to examine how the Dutch dealt with the consequences of the Second World War with special reference to the pensions and support for freedom fighters. Albie had instructed me to collect information for ANC constitutional negotiator Kader Asmal on justice and reconciliation in a number of countries. Then came this opportunity to visit Holland to see for myself how they had dealt with their past.

On the plane to Amsterdam, I block all unpleasant thoughts of my disintegrating marriage and settle in to enjoy the journey. This is the second time that I have left the country since 1990. Before that, I had never travelled abroad because the security police had withdrawn my passport in 1981, confining me to the country. Some people are fearful when this mighty machine takes to the skies but I have only ever felt a sense of exhilaration. Strongly influenced by my dad, I do not forget to say my prayers as the plane picks up speed on the runway. A'ūthu billāhi minashaytānirajīm. Bismillāhi rahmānirrahim . . .

I feel the thud of the wheels flicking up against the body of the plane once it has lifted itself, nose first into the air. My stomach tingles. I smile as I pray and give myself over to that sense that I am personally surging into the vast infinite universe and loving every minute of it.

I cannot miss Anna Hollander, nurse and volunteer anti-apartheid activist, waiting for me outside the arrival lounge. She is twirling around a small paper ANC flag on a short thin stick to catch my attention. She is the only one with a flag in her hand and a broad grin and I am right to assume that she has come to collect me.

Silver-grey hair, a warm black coat and a scarf flung around her neck. Across her arm is draped a large white coat and red scarf for me. My small form disappears somewhere inside that huge white shape but I am warm and grateful as we step outside into the icy morning air.

At home, in her comfortable two-room apartment, sleep is our first priority. I am happy to jump into the soft comfy bed she has prepared for me. "After lunch, I will show you around Amsterdam and help you buy tickets for the train," says Anna.

Warmly wrapped up, we leave the train station and walk along Amsterdam's famous canals. We stop outside a four-storey building that houses the Rijks Institute on War Documentation (RIOD). "This is where you must come tomorrow morning," she says.

Shortly after the end of the Second World War, the Dutch government established this documentary institute to research all aspects of the war years. The original notion was that it would complete its work within five years. It took Dutch researchers twenty-one years to write the history of the Netherlands during the war. And today, this four-storey building holds an archive of 10 000 maps, registers and books. It is the place where families come daily in search of information about their families, their past, and their personal history. Here they have access to German police archival material that could disclose that a family member had been a spy or had been tortured severely.

For the next week, I sift through copious documents looking for answers to the questions facing us. What did they do with collaborators? I realise their context is different from ours. The allies had won the war and conquered the enemy. We are talking to the enemy because neither side is able to take power.

"Power lies discarded in the streets," I had told Reuters cameraman Jimmy Mathews after my release in 1986. "They cannot take it back but we are not able to pick it up."

Our context is definitely different and I am mindful that I need to bear this in mind constantly. It is nevertheless fascinating to read about how a conquering nation has dealt with similar issues.

I take careful notes of the most interesting details that pop up at me. Special squads from the former resistance movement and the Netherlands

Military Administration arrested more than 120 000 people suspected of treason and collaboration. What would happen if we were to do this in our country? All those many people who worked with the apartheid government helping to suppress and oppress the vast majority.

The Dutch herded these persons into camps and held them under very poor conditions as they awaited trial. Committees consisting of local dignitaries and resistance fighters selected prisoners who were considered to be completely harmless and they were released. Soon, the number of internees proved a strong argument for moderation of punishment.

The post-war Dutch government considered the massive internment far too expensive for the completely impoverished country. Eventually in October and November 1945, it provided for decrees that made out-of-court settlements possible in the case of petty collaborators. At least 90 000 people were released in this way.

About 14 562 persons were convicted by Special Courts and 49 920 by Tribunals. Of those 14 562 convicted by Special Courts, 152 were condemned to death and over 14 000 to imprisonment. The numbers stagger me. If this was the case in Holland, I wonder what happened in neighbouring European countries? How many people were brought to justice for their role in the Second World War?

As the saga unravels, I sense how they moved towards considering pardons for the offenders. Barely two years after the war in 1947, the then minister of justice implemented a policy of pardoning extended by subsequent ministers until 1952.

I pay particular attention to the pension laws for resistance fighters because I know this is a huge issue back home.

After the war, the Dutch government passed a law allowing generous pension payouts to those who suffered at least ten percent disability as a result of their actions. In the case of eighty percent or greater disability, an extra allowance was paid to the applicant over and above the pension already received. Many years were to pass before consideration was given to pensions and compensations to other categories of war victims.

Peter Romijn, director of RIOD, generously provides numerous documents that I can take home with me. Mieke van Bree, Anna's neighbour, helps to translate the Dutch pieces so that I can understand the content fully.

My notebooks are full and stacks of papers weigh down my suitcase.

I call home to speak with Ruschka.

"Have you bought my Barbie doll, mom," she says.

"Not yet, darling, but I won't forget," I say.

"Mom, please don't bring me a black Barbie with black hair. I want one with blonde hair and blue eyes."

I am taken aback. It seems my daughter at age six has me figured. I have been looking around for a Barbie that would look a little more like she does but clearly I have got it wrong. I will have to swallow hard and buy one of those insipid dolls that cost the earth. I think about my recent trip to Utrecht, where I saw this beautiful doll in a shop window. Not one that is thin like a reed, unnatural, unlike a real woman. This doll had long brown hair, brown eyes, a full firm body and could be tucked up into bed next to Ruschka at night. I had a doll like that when I was a child.

As I put down the phone, I think to myself: Well, I have to buy this Barbie but I am also going to buy that doll I saw. If Ruschka does not want it, I will keep it for myself.

Anna has taken off from work so that we can travel to Stigting '45, the national centre for medico-psychological treatment for members of the resistance and victims of the war in Oegstgeest. Institutionalised care for the victims came as late as 1972, nearly thirty years after the war. The government was forced to provide the support when controversy raged as they made preparation to release three Nazi war criminals held in the Netherlands. Sympathy for war victims ran high and concerned activists were able to press for official care. The original institution was a private foundation that raised money from the public for the purposes of granting stipends to those in need. Little priority was given to how the ordeals suffered during the war could be dealt with psychologically.

It is a rainy day and Anna turns the wipers on to fast mode as we stop at a traffic light.

"This evening, I will introduce you to my walking partner," she says.

Anna was married for ten years then left her husband. She has no children. Now she says she has come to the conclusion that one person cannot fulfil her different needs. I am astonished when she keeps on introducing me to different partners. There is one she goes travelling with. There is another she goes to movies with and another one who is her sexual partner. For me, this is all rather funny. My marriage is falling apart right now and finding another partner is not high on my agenda. In fact, I hardly trust my judgement and am eager just to be on my own, to protect myself.

I laugh at Anna's stories. For me to fully grasp what she is saying I would have to turn my world upside down and it is too soon for that.

"I have to go home and sort out my divorce," I say. "I don't know how this is going to happen because I am married by Muslim rites and in South Africa Muslim marriages are not legally recognised."

"So, does this mean that you are not legally married?"

"Yes, in the eyes of the law of the land. But in the eyes of God, I am. I really do not know how it's all going to work. I'll face it when I get there."

She parks carefully in an empty parking bay in front of Stigting '45. She hands me an umbrella and I smile. Anna is so thoughtful. She has come well prepared with an umbrella for each one of us.

We are ushered into an office where I interview the resident counsellor.

She takes us on a tour of the centre and I look through the glass window of a lounge door where people are gathered together in little groups. They range in age from forty-eight to ninety years and have come to seek relief for pain they have been carrying inside themselves for many years. Some are war victims, but some are the children of those who were traumatised by the war.

I stop outside a small room painted in soft pink. On the bed is a fluffy stuffed dog cheerfully resting its head on the pink pillowcase. On the bedside table is an array of toiletries, perfumes and soaps neatly arranged as if they are in display on a shop counter.

"This is occupied by one of our clients whose mother witnessed the bombing of their town," she says. "She suddenly could no longer carry on with her work and the doctors sent her here to us because her trauma is linked to the war."

I suddenly feel very vulnerable and desperately in need of care. Oh would it not be wonderful to snuggle down into those soft pink sheets and block out the world? My heart is beating rather fast in my chest. I think of myself and then all the comrades back home. What a difference it would make to us if we had such a facility. I am tempted to burrow in but then at the same time I feel irritated and angry by the lavishness of it all. How can there be such disparity in the world that a few people are given such great care and so many are given no care at all?

I vaguely hear my host speaking: "People come here for day visits but others stay up to a year. We have twenty-four beds. And in the last half of this year (1992), 450 people passed through the clinic weekly.

As she speaks, a woman passes us and enters the room with the fluffy dog. She had observed her mother's trauma. She was born at the end of the war and yet forty-five years later, she is the one who has to deal with its consequences.

I don't know how I am going to do it, but I vow now that I must find a way not to do this to my daughter. Albie is right. We have to break the cycle. But this is not only a collective responsibility, I have to break my own cycle and I have absolutely no idea how I will do it. As we turn to leave, I take the image of that woman into my heart, carrying her with me as a constant reminder that this is not the kind of future any of us should wish for our daughters.

CHAPTER FOURTEEN

W̰e are like two strangers sitting next to one another. There is a gap big enough to place another chair between us. He does not look at me and I have the same difficulty with him. He is the father of my child, a man who has known me intimately for the past ten years. Yet I am about to put a signature on a piece of paper that will forever sever my marital relationship with him. I am painfully aware that it is the marital relationship that I am about to end but not the relationship. He will always be in my life and I in his because of our daughter Ruschka and a signature can never wipe that away.

She adores her father and there is no way that I will deprive her of him. But right now, I cannot consider what all this is going to mean practically. I am facing what many Muslim women are experiencing, a talaaq (an Islamic divorce procedure). The most important thing for me now is just to get the paperwork done. It reminds me of the day my parents gave consent for me to marry.

Johnny was banned and had just been released from prison. He had been inside for breaking his banning order. A traditional wedding was out of the question. We would be married by Muslim rites but before the ceremony, he had to convert to Islam. In terms of my religion I could not marry a non-Muslim man who was not prepared to convert. Off he went to a local imām who introduced him to the basic teachings of Islam. What amazed me was that the weight of this conversion fell entirely on my shoulders. The greatest concern of the local community appeared to be an assurance that he had changed his name – something that I later discovered was not an absolute requirement but voluntary.

For this other, sadder occasion, we meet at the offices of the Muslim Judicial Council and Sheikh Nazeem is in the room with us. He is waiting for a second sheikh to witness the process and tries in his own way to set us at ease.

"This will not take long. You just have to sign as soon as the witness comes."

A few weeks ago, I had gone to see him to find out how to go about obtaining a divorce by muslim rites.

"Did he hit you?" he had asked.

"No."

"Did he fail to provide for you?"

"No."

"Well, what is the problem?"

I had explained that I did not want to discuss the detail of why I wanted a divorce.

"I think that would be a matter for the two of us."

"You cannot apply for a divorce giving no reason," he had said. "The only way we can give you a divorce is if you and he appear in front of a panel of imāms so that we can hear the different sides of the story. We could then decide whether a divorce is necessary."

This was not something I had wanted to do.

"Is there any other way that I can get this divorce, Sheikh?"

"Well, if he applies for the divorce, it will be straightforward. Ask him to apply and then we just have to get together to sign the papers."

It transpired that the man can ask for a divorce while the women can ask for an annulment (faskh) on certain grounds.

I had had to ask him. The thought of appearing in front of a panel of imāms had not appealed to me. The only other time in my life when I had had a similar experience had been when I was eleven years old and was publicly tested on the Holy Qur'ān and special Islamic subjects. Fourteen of us had walked through the streets of Wynberg carrying our Qur'āns, followed by hundreds of children belonging to our madressa. I had been too young to be bothered by the enormity of the exercise and had merrily recited the verses I had been asked to in front of a hall packed with people upstairs and in every room downstairs. The older students had been more aware of the pressure of the panel of imāms they had to face and some had been quite tearful as they waited their turns to be tested.

I had asked Johnny and he had obliged. Neither of us had been charmed at the idea of having our personal problems aired in public.

So here we are, waiting to sign the papers.

The door opens and in steps an imām whose name I do not know. But I recognise his face. He greets us and smiles. Sheikh places the papers in front of my husband and indicates where he should sign. He signs.

He then moves the papers over to me and I sign. He signs and the witness signs. He shuffles the papers together, thanks the witness – who leaves – and then turns his attention to Johnny.

"You are a free man," he says grinning. Free, by implication, to take another woman. Johnny understands the implication and they both smile.

I can see Sheikh is expecting me to react but I say nothing. He turns to me.

"You can go to work for the next three months, but you cannot attend any social function until you have your third period. Once you have your third period, you must let me know and then your divorce will be final. This will give both of you time to consider if you still want to reconcile. If you reconcile within the three months, then this divorce falls away."

He pauses, again as if he expects me to react.

I am not going to react. There is a time and place for everything and this is not the time to make a stand for all womankind. I just want this divorce.

I have no problem with the notion that I must refrain from social interaction, in other words from sexual activity, for the next three months. I have never been able to understand how people rush from one relationship to another. I know myself and need the time to heal.

My difficulty is that I find it unacceptable that this rule is applied only to the woman. How wonderful it would be if it applied to both male and female. The couple could use the time to contemplate their relationship and come to a final decision about whether they wanted each other or not. This would make sense. From the male point of view, the present practice does make sense. Religiously, the woman has to stay secluded so that the man can determine whether she is carrying his child or not. She should also stay secluded so that she is not contaminated by another relationship should her husband want to return to her in this time. How convenient!

My dad always says that we will see change over time and should not be overly worried. In his seventy-three years, he has seen many changes. Some religious rituals that he grew up with and that he believed were stipulated by the Almighty are no longer practised.

My mother likes to tell the story of a person who was one of the first in Cape Town whose body was placed in a motorised vehicle and driven to the cemetery. The story is recorded in the *Muslim News* of 1961. Muslims of the Cape carried their dead on their shoulders to their burial grounds and depended on their physical strength and no other means of transport. To place the body in a vehicle was a notion unheard of forty years ago, but it has become increasingly routine today.

I hope that I will live to see the day when a sense of equality and fairness permeate all the rituals of a religion I hold very dear. Experience has taught me that this will not come automatically. It will require persistent pressure from enlightened women and men the world over to chip away at the notion that devotion to the ancient rules in itself guarantees a path to pure religious practice. If I don't see it, I pray my daughter will.

I ask Sheikh if I can be excused.

"Do I still have to do anything else?" I say.

"No."

I cannot bring myself to shake his hand or that of my former husband. "Assalāmu alaykum."

"Wa alaykum salām," says Sheikh.

I turn awkwardly towards the door, clutch the knob tightly as I open it and flee through the reception area out into the deserted parking lot. I half-run, half-walk to the car, eager to get away. I am aware that this is one of the most important moments of my life. I am taking leave of an experience of my youth. I expect to feel sad but I am not. I am happy that I have had the strength to admit that this has not worked for me. My bottom thumps onto the leather seat as I swing myself into the car. Thud. I have hit the bottom of a slippery slide in the park and am relieved to find myself sitting, dazed but in one piece, on the gravel landing.

We did not own a home or much in the way of material possessions so there was nothing major to discuss about sharing assets. We had each one been contributing equally to running the household and held no monies in joint accounts.

In some senses, it has been logistically quite simple. I took my child and a suitcase of clothes on one day. Then sent my brother to fetch my computer the next. We shared a few of the household utensils and that was it.

But deep inside all three of us, the wounds were deep.

"Mom, I have just finished my third period," I say.

"You should call Sheikh and tell him," says my mom.

"What should I say: Sheikh, I am just calling to tell you that I have had my third period?" I say.

She looks at me and then sees my smile. We both laugh.

I shake my head. "Mom, I leave this one to you. You call him if you would like to but I am certainly not going to."

I can see she is not going to do it. "How about getting dad to do it?" Her eyes crinkle up as do mine and our laughter rings through the kitchen, bringing Ruschka up the three small steps leading from the yard into the house.

"Mom! Gran!" She looks from the one to the other, her tight little cheeks move up against her eyes as she grins and throws her arms around my waist. Still laughing, I silently thank God and her dad for giving me this precious gift.

I sweep her up in my arms and carry her off for her evening bath. She wants Mieke, the doll with the long brown hair, brown eyes and sturdy body I had bought for her in Holland. Mieke too will have to be washed and prepared for bed. The fancy Barbie she insisted I buy is stuck in the cupboard in a shoe-box, dressed to the nines with no name. Later, she will demand that Mieke be tucked up with her when she lolls off to sleep. After all, whoever gets into bed eager to cuddle a Barbie doll?

CHAPTER FIFTEEN

It's an awkward moment. We are not quite able to look at each other. I am fussing over Ruschka. He takes the camera from the car as I lead her to him. She is dressed in a pink and white striped dress with buttons down the front. She wears white socks and brown shoes, completing the school uniform. Her friend Waldo hops out of the car to stand next to her for this special photograph. Johnny has brought him along so that he can record their first day at school. Waldo has on grey short pants, a white shirt, a striped tie and a navy school blazer. He with his hair cropped short against his head, she with a mop of short dark curls. They both have their school bags on their backs.

We had had quite a debate about where to send Ruschka to school. I wanted to send her to Fairview Primary in Grassy Park because of its excellent reputation and because my sister's children were at that school. The principal, Mr Christians, had been my standard five teacher at Douglas Road Primary School and I had the greatest respect for his teaching abilities. Johnny argued that we should send her to Plumstead Preparatory School, a formerly white school but now open to all. As the children prepare for the moment their image will be frozen in time, the debate about their education runs through my head in a timeless loop.

"I don't want my child to come home speaking like a white child," I say. "I also don't want her to struggle with feeling inferior amongst a whole lot of white children."

"But we struggled to open the schools and it is up to us to make sure that they are racially mixed," he says. "At first, it will be difficult but after a while more and more children will come and there will be quite a mix."

I remembered how I felt coming to UCT and seeing white students for the first time. I had grown up in a Coloured area and attended a Coloured school and suddenly to be flung into the sea of whites was a frightening and intimidating experience.

"Why don't we let her go to a mixed school when she goes to high school? By then, she would be sure of her identity and more confident," I say.

We considered all the options but in the end I had to concede that her

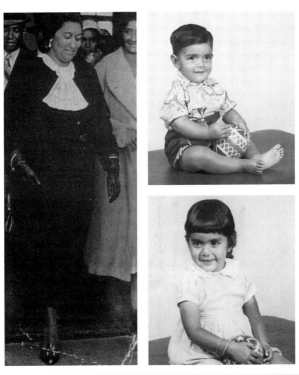

Top left: My maternal grandmother, Gadija Hendricks, way back in the 1940s.
Top right: My brother Mansoor and I as young children.
Bottom: My mom and dad, shortly after their marriage in 1944.

Top: My mom, on the far right, with her mother and sisters.
Bottom: Imām Abdullah Haron, his wife Galima and two of their children, Moegamat and
    Shamila.

Right: Sheikh Nazeem Mohammed at a local function in the
early 1960s, with Imām
Haron behind him.
Bottom: Imām Haron, the editor
of *Muslim Views* and associated with the Pan African
Congress (PAC) in the 1960s.

(Courtesy of the Haron family)

RASHID LOMBARD

Top: A twenty-year-old Albie Sachs standing at the press table as the police invade the Congress of the People at Kliptown in 1955.

Bottom left: Zora Mehlomakhulu with her daughter Nosizwe, after spending four months in detention in 1976.

Bottom right: Mildred Ramakaba-Lesiea, one of the key organisers of women in the Western Cape.

Ashley Kriel, the Ché Guevara of the Cape Flats.

RASHID LOMBARD

RASHID LOMBARD

Top: Ruschka's nine-year-old sister Leila, speaking on behalf of her banned father at the launch of the UDF on 20 August 1983, in front of a capacity crowd of 15 000 at the Rocklands Civic Centre. Alan Boesak and Archie Gumede are looking on.

Bottom: A rare moment when I saw Johnny in hiding, with his children Ruschka, Leila, Yasser and Fidel. With us are Yana, Shadley and Chevan Lombard.

RASHID LOMBARD

Top: My brother Adam and his wife Zerene (Shirley) with their son Reyhaan moments after he stepped out of Victor Verster Prison in Paarl.

Bottom: Elizabeth Erasmus, minus her black-green-and-gold beads, marches to police headquarters to demand the release of Shirley Gunn. Behind her is my mom and other Wynberg women.

Top left: At the A.M.E. Church in Hazendal, Athlone, Graeme Bloch, himself banned for several years, announces that UDF leaders will defy their banning orders as part of a defiance campaign in 1987.

Top Right: Veteran trade unionist Oscar Mpetha who was released on bail of one rand, while facing charges of incitement.

Bottom: Myself with Govan Mbeki and his doctor, Mamisa Chabula, shortly before leaving for New York in 1995.

father's argument was superior to mine. I could not allow fear to be the source of influencing such an important decision.

Ruschka and Waldo's excitement ease the awkwardness of the moment. Waldo gets into the car with Uncle Johnny and Ruschka gets into the car with me and off we go.

The school is just down the road in the neighbouring suburb of Plumstead. It's funny when I think of it – this is the first time that I feel comfortable coming into this suburb even though it is right next to my home. There was always some kind of invisible line drawn across the boundary road preventing us from venturing into shops. I notice that the streets are tree-lined and pavement lawns neatly tended by the local council. Wherever you go in South Africa, it is easy to identify areas designated for whites. They have trees, well-laid out roads, grassed parks with swings for children to play on, good street lighting and well-developed shopping complexes.

I park the car in an adjacent street and walk around the corner towards the school grounds. Plumstead Preparatory is a small school where children come for their first three years of schooling. I thought it was a very good idea for Ruschka to be in a space where she is not immediately confronted with big children. I take her to the school gate, bend down to kiss her and wish her well for this new adventure.

"Enjoy, sweetie pie. I will fetch you at lunchtime."

She is not clinging onto me as she did when she first went to pre-school. This child of mine is ready for school and quick to say goodbye. She turns momentarily, waves to me and then walks towards the school entrance. I wait until her little body disappears in a sea of pink as the pupils move through the open doors into the spacious school corridors.

The first term has ended and we are getting ready to spend a few days at the beach. Ruschka insists that we should pack the large Easter egg that her father brought her last night.

"Tomorrow is Easter, mom. I must take the Easter egg."

"Ruschka, we have enough things to carry. Remember, we will have to carry everything down those steps," I say.

"It's OK, mom. I'll run up and down."

Ruschka and her friend Zeenat hop into the back seat. I pack our bags into the boot and reverse the car out of the driveway into the short back street. Zeenat has taken Waldo's place. She is the daughter of my neighbour and cannot stay away from Ruschka. They are always together. It suits me fine because it means that I am left alone to read. The minute Ruschka is on her own, all her attention turns to me. That's the problem with having a single child. I have come to realise that rearing a number of children at the same time is easier because they keep each other busy. I no longer wonder how my mom coped with six of us.

We wind our way across the mountain and down towards Clifton beach. Albie is renting a bungalow there where he lives permanently now and he has a room in the basement where we will be spending the Easter weekend.

Lugging haversacks and carrier bags of food down these steps is not at all a fun thing to do. I wonder how Albie manages with his one arm. But the pristine beached cove down below makes the effort worthwhile.

Albie is as delighted to see us as we are to see him. He hands us the key to the downstairs room and we move in.

"I want to invite some friends around to spend the day with us on the beach tomorrow," I say. "Will this be alright?"

"Do whatever you would like to do," he says.

"I am seeing some people in the morning but will be free to meet with your friends in the afternoon," he says.

Ruschka and Zeenat cannot wait to go down to the beach. "It's too cold to swim this afternoon," I say to them. "Take your buckets and spades and build a castle."

We run down the last flight of stairs separating the bungalow from the beach below. Rocks protrude through the surface of the sand, breaking the soft smoothness of the long white stretch. As the winter comes, the sea draws the sand into its belly, leaving the huge boulders naked under grey skies. At the first signs of spring, each wave brings with it a blanket of sand piling up one on top of the other until the beach is restored to its summer smoothness.

The water is cold but I cannot resist taking off my shoes and walking along the edge of the waves breaking on the seashore. I roll up the bottom of my pants so that the cold wet edges do not flap against my bare skin. A hot shower after this walk will help me sleep well tonight.

Ruschka and Zeenat are digging a trench around the castle, their hands and arms covered in sand. "Mom, come and help us," says Ruschka.

I kneel down beside them, feeling the damp grains against my knees, and help remove the little mounds of sand blocking the trench. The autumn sun warms the back of my neck and I smile as I watch their serious faces concentrating intensely on their major task. This weekend, I want to be like them, working with the sand, aware only of the pleasant sounds of the screeching gulls, immersing myself completely in the now, forgetting about the past and unconcerned about the future.

We are into the third year of negotiations. It's taking so much longer than we had expected and it's all so very distant from us. I am fortunate that I work closely with Albie and hear more about the process than is being reported in the newspapers. But for most of us who have been intimately involved in bringing about the situation that made negotiations possible, the waiting requires a great deal of patience. We are fortunate that those at the negotiating table are greatly respected and largely trusted by most in the democratic movement. I hate to think of what may happen if that trust breaks down. I sometimes have that niggling feeling that perhaps we trust too much and that leaders in many countries throughout history have been sidetracked at crucial moments.

"Mom," says Ruschka. "You said you were going to help us with the castle."

"Yes, yes, I am."

I start digging again, feeling guilty that the activity cannot hold my mind in the present. I want to immerse myself in this castle but I seem to float so easily down its moat into a world of politics as I worry about how the negotiations are going to work out.

"Dig, mom. Dig." Ruschka brings me back to the beach, the gulls and an awareness of the rough feel of the sand in my hands. What's the point of making elaborate arrangements to carry clothes and food down to the beach for a few days so that we can take a break and then I carry the world down here with me? I have to make a huge effort to help my mind focus on my environment – the natural beauty and the variety of beach-goers meandering along the shore. This is one of the beaches we never knew about and could never come to. Maiden's Cove next door had been reserved for non-whites and it was the only small space on the Camps Bay coastline that we had been familiar with as children.

Last year it had been such a treat when I had come to Camps Bay beach on New Year's day. It is a beach just further on from this one and very famous for its soft white sands, tall palm trees and bikini-clad young women. The scenes on that day had been very different from the ones the international tourist set are used to. There had been people of all colours and classes filling every space on the wide expanse of sand. Pretty beach umbrellas with sunbathing holiday-makers had been dotted along one side but the strip of grass on the border of the beach had been covered with mothers and fathers surrounded by children, uncles, aunts brought to the beach by local taxis. They had come with their pots of food, tins of biscuits and portable music systems blasting forth the popular sounds of Brenda Fassie. Beer flowed freely and the eating was continuous.

Here on Albie's beach, I am expecting various friends and my brother Mansoor, his wife Kayzuran and children to join us. Once they come, I will be able to leave the girls with them and go up to the bungalow to prepare some food.

"Aunty Beida!" I look up and see Haroon running towards us. Following a short distance behind is his mother, Shirley, a friend and comrade. They are the first to arrive.

Haroon is five years old and after throwing his arms around my neck, his attention is immediately on Ruschka and Zeenat and their castle.

"We need some shells, Haroon," says Ruschka.

"What do you want to do with the shells?" he asks.

"We want to put the shells against the wall we are building around the castle to make it strong," says Zeenat.

"Go with her and collect some shells," says Ruschka. She is taking charge and giving orders. I suppose with a mother and a father both with that inclination, what could be expected? It is a strength that needs to be tempered with large doses of compassion for it to become a positive feature of her interactions with others.

Shirley is excited. We are expecting a number of comrades who were in the underground with her. The thought of spending time together under such relaxed conditions is pleasant.

Ben is coming. But Ben is no longer Ben. I have known him by his fighter name but his real name is Shanil.

My back feels comfortable as it relaxes against a boulder. I pick up my book, which lies on a towel, and settle in to read as Shirley joins the children in their hunt for pretty shells. Every moment I have to spare, I read *An Instant in the Wind*. Andre Brink has me completely enthralled. He is one of my favourite South African authors and as I plough through the middle of the book, I am fast considering giving this the status of my favourite title.

100

I am a sucker for human drama that knits together romance, history and politics. *An Instant in the Wind* describes with great detail the trek of a white South African woman into the South African interior accompanied by a local black slave. As I read I cannot but marvel at the use of language, the composition of sentences and the graphic description of vivid scenes, bringing alive the natural beauty of the Cape.

"I want to be a writer, not just a reporter," I had told Albie shortly after I had first met him. "I want to learn how to take my writing onto another level beyond all boundaries I have known before."

The best way to do this, I know, is to write and to surround myself with those who write and their work. I glance up from my book and see Ben waving in the distance. I wave back and get up ready to hug him as he reaches me.

"Gosh, Ben, I must get used to calling you by your real name."

He laughs in his soft, gentle way. He is a quiet young man, a teacher by profession and a committed member of MK. With the cease-fire agreed to two years ago, he has slowly been able to pick up the pieces of a ruptured life. During the late eighties, I had only ever seen Ben at night in cars slipped into parking garages.

I have to put my book away now because more comrades come trundling along through the sand. Soon we are a large group chattering away and pleased to be together under such different circumstances.

"Albie will be ready to join us before the sun sets," I say. "I am going to go up so long to start the fire and then you must decide who will braai."

The fire is going along one side of the bungalow by the time they all trot in. I have to warn the children not to walk into Albie's room with their sandy feet. Various parents take care of bathing their offspring in the room downstairs that I share with the kids. By the time they are all spruced up in their pyjamas, we are putting the finishing touches to the evening meal.

The last few pieces of marinated meat are placed on the hot coals as the steel tray filled with cooked meat is slipped into the oven to keep warm. Shirley is making the salad, my brother Mansoor is helping to finish the braai and Shanil is stacking paper plates, cutlery and condiments onto a small table in Albie's one-bedroomed studio. My friend Anu, who has come all the way from Johannesburg to spend the weekend with me, is lounging in a deck-chair on the balcony.

Albie says the children can come upstairs to watch television in his bedroom after supper and I can see Ruschka is very pleased. She knows that we will interrupt them when the news is on but other than that the television is all theirs. As our country lurches from one dramatic moment to another, we are acutely conscious that any news bulletin can bring an unexpected crisis.

But it has been a quiet Easter Saturday with the usual campers and family outings around the country and we can settle down to a fun-filled evening.

My brother Mansoor, the baby in our family, has brought his guitar along and Albie has loads of CDs. We get the children to join in as we sing at the top of our voices. Mansoor, with his languid dark eyes set in his bearded face, has this funny habit of putting his own words into popular songs. He is particularly fond of replacing names with the names of people we know. Instead of singing "Mona Lisa, Mona Lisa, how I love you", he chooses a local name that is phonetically similar:

"Gayru Nisa, Gayru Nisa, how I love you," he sings, leaving us in stitches whenever a name change corresponds to somebody in the room. If I were to say exactly the same thing he says, it would not be so funny. He has that special knack that my dad had passed on to the male members of our family. Both my sister, Julie, and I are seriously joking-challenged. We cannot pull it off.

Then he comes with the old Cape slave songs that we all know so well.

"Hoe lekker slaan die goema.
Goema, goema, goema
Goema van tant Sarah."

I beat my hands on the table top in tune with the guitar as we did when we were children. I remember how my eldest brother, Yusuf, used to beat out the tunes on my mother's biscuit tins. There were many nights when the whole family got together making music in whichever way we could – clapping our hands together, beating biscuit tins and testing the sound of a spoon against another spoon, or on the table top or against the rim of a glass.

In later years, Mansoor learned to play the guitar and added a bit of class to our rather amateur efforts.

"Goodness, we are making such a lot of noise," I say. "Are we not going to disturb these neighbours?"

"We may be," says Albie.

I had seen the next door neighbour, Ivor Garb, on his balcony earlier so

I knew he was at home. What on earth would he be thinking about this racket coming from Albie's place?

"Tell him to come over," shouts somebody in the group. "Yes, if he is here with us, he won't mind if we are making a noise."

I giggle, pretty certain that this was not the done thing in Clifton. We are used to being in and out of each others homes in Wynberg or Bo-Kaap or Athlone but I had a good idea that this would not be the practice here.

Anyway, I am game. I have met Ivor before so I take up the challenge.

"I am going next door to get him," I say, and everybody laughs.

Five minutes later, I am back with a grey-haired Ivor by my side and I can see the general look of disbelief on their faces.

"Mr Ivor Garb to the company," I say.

It does not take long before Ivor gets into the mood singing ditties from his childhood.

He leaves well after midnight with most of the comrades and when Anu and I settle down to sleep the bungalow seems still to vibrate with the happy sounds that have bounced back and forth off the walls all evening.

By the time everybody wakes up, I am preparing breakfast upstairs so that we can all eat together. I can see Albie is very happy to have all this company. He usually lives by himself and I am intrigued to see that he enjoys a full house.

We are about to eat when the telephone rings. Albie walks over to his desk, sits down on the chair and picks up the handset. The elbow of his left arm rests on the desk while his short right arm hangs loosely against his body. "Yes," he says. I am chatting to Anu.

"Oh no!"

We stop talking.

"When?"

He listens.

"Give me ten minutes."

He slowly moves the handset down onto its cradle and falls forward onto the desk with his left arm serving as a cushion, his short right arm squeezed up tightly against the side of his chest. "NO. NO. NO!"

Oh dear God. Something must have happened to his mother. Or to one of his two sons. I am not quite sure what to do.

What could it be?

I cannot find the right words.

Before I can say anything, he lifts up his head, turns his anguished body towards us, with tears in his eyes and says: "Chris Hani has been assassinated."

Where? Who? How? Can this be true?

"That was the BBC. They want to interview me about his death," he says.

My heart twists and the tears well up in my eyes. Chris. Oh Chris. It cannot be. That broad ready smile, the large high forehead with its cushion of hair, the affable yet formidable freedom fighter. The natural successor to Mandela, the president-in-waiting, he was one of the key leaders who held together the fine ends of a tenuous peace process, the one who was the glimmer of hope the day Ashley died.

I stand in the middle of that room, unable to move, to fling my arms around Albie or Anu, to express my grief and to soothe theirs.

A pain grows in my chest and I become aware of a strong feeling of the impending danger. It is as if I have just had word that the banks of the Olifants River have burst and I am living in a cottage on a luscious green orange farm in Citrusdal right in the path of the tide of water sweeping down the valley.

Albie must take the BBC call. Anu is tearful. I have to go home too and see other comrades to hear what has to be done. Our planned weekend is coming to an abrupt end. "Ruschie, you and Zeenat pack up. We have to go home."

"But mom, you said we will stay until Monday."

Understandably, she does not appreciate the enormity of the news we have just heard. I lower my voice and say to her softly: "Ruschie, I am sorry darling, but we must go home."

She looks disappointed but does not argue, climbs through the hatch in the floor, down the steep wooden ladder and into the room below. Zeenat follows dutifully.

I turn on the radio so that we can hear the eleven o'clock news. For once I am not easily able to flip into organising mode. I don't know what we are going to do to prevent the country from sliding into chaos. Not as I hear the detail.

More than 9 000 political killings over the past three years have not prepared us for this. He was shot four times at about 10.15 a.m. as he stepped out of the car he had just parked in the driveway of his home in Boksburg, a conservative white Johannesburg suburb. His shattered body was lying in a pool of congealing blood on the family driveway. He was without his bodyguards on a rare day off and planning to attend this afternoon's historic soccer match between South Africa and Mauritius. He is no more.

An hour later, I am with the comrades when we hear that a suspect has been arrested. Less than an hour after the shooting, police arrested a man at a nearby shopping center. Neighbours had seen a red car speed from the scene of the accident. Police have identified the suspect as Janus Wallus, right-winger of Polish descent. He was believed to have had two guns with him.

I am in my slippers and nightgown. My hair is uncombed and I have not gotten around to taking a bath this morning. All I want to do is sit here and watch the television screen to see his body lying in state. Mansoor and other comrades have travelled to Johannesburg to attend the funeral but for once it is just too much of an ordeal for me. It was a wonderful surprise to hear that the proceedings would be televised live. As images of the body in its white coffin come flashing across the screen, I call Ruschka to come and see. She sits for a few minutes and then is up again and off to play. I want her to watch but I know it would not be a good idea to insist. Often, children of activists become totally disinterested in the cause of their parents after they have been dragged like reluctant horses to the water-trough once too often.

The funeral is on for the whole morning and she pops in and out. That is good enough for me. My energy has deserted me. I have only enough in me to focus on the proceedings.

When Dimpo Hani speaks, her dark sunglasses hiding her red eyes, I finally break down and cry.

"I want to thank you, Chris, for nineteen glorious years . . ." she says.

All my pent-up emotions of the past two weeks come rushing to the fore. I cry for her, for her children, for our country and also for myself. But as the camera pans over the crowded stadium showing both stands and lawns covered with people paying their last respects, the tears subside as I am filled with a sense of pride in the movement that so many of us have helped to build. His death had provoked marches in towns across the country and, unfortunately, considerable chaos in some instances where looters went on the rampage.

Despite the terrible loss, our leaders have shown a maturity over this period that carries within it seeds of hope. What an experience it was a few nights ago to see Nelson Mandela go on national television addressing the nation. The apartheid leadership stood powerless as the country teetered on the brink of anarchy. De Klerk had no choice but to stand aside and allow

Mandela to speak directly through the apartheid-controlled broadcaster, sending an unspoken message that power no longer resided with the old order.

Winning permission to televise the funeral was also a major coup for the liberation movement, reinforcing this message but at the same time providing a mechanism to make possible the participation of millions in the collective outpouring of grief gripping the nation.

Ruschka runs into the room just as Dimpo releases a white dove into the air, symbolising a commitment to the peace process for which Chris had sacrificed so much. "Look, mummy, it's flying," she says. Another comrade releases a small group of doves that follow Dimpo's dove into the air. They hover, then glide through the air as the coffin is lowered into the grave. "They are flying away, mom. They are flying away."

As I watch them fly, I cannot help feeling that peace is escaping from our clutches.

The next morning, I turn on the radio as I wake from a restless sleep and feel my tight strained face relax into a soft happy smile.

Dimpo's dove with the others had flown back in the night and are perched on Chris's grave.

CHAPTER SIXTEEN

It's a cold rainy day in the Cape. I look for umbrellas to carry with me to the polling station. They are usually in the broom cupboard. Ruschka must have put them somewhere in her room. My head is burrowed into the jerseys stacked at the bottom of her cupboard when I hear my dad's voice as he comes through the back door. I raise my head as he walks into the bedroom. His face is flushed, his eyes sparkling.

"You must see the long queues all over," he says. "It will take us hours to vote here in Wynberg. Perhaps you should go a little later. People are not even bothering about the rain. They keep on coming."

I have come home for the day to cast my vote in my neighbourhood. Special arrangements were made for us to vote yesterday in Johannesburg where I am working but I had to come home.

Today, today is the day. At seventy-four, my dad will cast his vote for the first time. Thank God that he has lived to see this day. So many have not. So many who have longed for citizenship and worked for it will not share in this moment. As he walks ahead of me through the bedroom, my small lounge and into the kitchen, I detect a youthful jauntiness in his stride that I have not seen for a long while. If he were to hop and skip like a small boy in front of me now, it would not surprise me. I cannot help smiling.

"I am going to Grassy Park to see what's happening there," he says, leaving me to welcome my mom and eldest brother, Yusuf. Warmly dressed in jerseys, they are armed with umbrellas and eager to walk to the civic centre a few blocks away.

We wave goodbye to my dad as he hops into his car.

Long lines snake from the entrance to the civic center in numerous curves across the expansive car-park. Women and men, black and white, with caps, hats, scarves and coats. Colourful umbrellas dot the endless line of eager voters.

What a sight! We have to stay here now. I am not interested in coming back when the lines are shorter. I am standing here however long it takes to get to that polling booth. With my mom and brother next to me, I step out of line to survey the voters. Some I recognise. Others are from the neighbouring white suburb. Labourers in their faded wind-breakers and peaked caps, local teachers enjoying a break from school, domestic workers from the surrounding white suburbs with their white employers for once standing in the same line to vote.

After two hours, Yusuf wanders off and comes back to the line armed with a salomie (a flat bread wrapped around mince curry). He walks up and down the line chatting to neighbours known to him from his childhood days. I call him back as we near the entrance to the voting station. After another hour of waiting, I finally enter the hall. An official leads me to the table where I produce my identity document. My thumb is dipped in ink to prevent me from voting a second time. I am shown to a row of kiosks where I look at the ballot paper through a haze. It seems so unreal. I find Madiba's face and make my cross next to his party. He is smiling. I smile back at him as I lift the paper from the hardboard surface.

I have chosen him and his party to be the caretakers of the democracy that we all fought for. If he and his party destroys that trust, we will find other caretakers. I hope that it is understood that we fought not for the freedom of a political party but for the freedom of South Africa to belong to all who live in it – for all to be treated fairly, not to be discriminated against or unfairly exploited.

The ANC has been the only party capable of uniting a broad range of South Africans and for now it has my vote. Should it betray that trust, there are many of us who will not hesitate to mobilise opposition using the organisational knowledge in which we are expertly schooled.

I fold the paper as I walk towards the next table. My mom is ahead of me plopping her ballot paper into the box. Then it's my turn. Behind me is my brother and, watching us, officially on duty, are a number of local neighbourhood acquaintances grinning from ear to ear.

As I look at the snake of people winding its way through the large hall, pushing their votes into the ballot box, I think about the moment when I switched on the television yesterday and saw the first South African casting her vote. In Wellington, New Zealand, where the sun rises nearly twelve hours earlier, Dr Nomaza Paintin, fifty, dressed in a black, green and gold dress, walks towards the ballot box holding her folded ballot paper in her hand. The announcer records that she is a niece of the president-in-waiting, Nelson Mandela. She raises her hand and pauses, conscious of the cameras and making history. She slowly lowers her hand and carefully inserts the paper into the slot. Click. Click. Click. The cameras flash, recording this historic moment. Tears come flowing down my cheeks. My jaw tightens. I bite my lip as my heart races. I want to scream. Why did so many people have to die, so many have their lives destroyed for this woman to slip a piece of paper into a box? The moment passes. The tears wash away the anger, creating space for excitement.

My mom, with my warm blue shawl over her shoulders, smiling, laughing, greeting, waving, brings me back into the voting hall. "Now I need a cup of tea. Let's get going."

Back home, the kitchen of my two-roomed apartment fills up with family, friends and their children. Ruschka is happily running around with the colourful election posters propped up against the washing line pole in our yard. A huge arrangement of flowers arrives from my personal assistant. She is in Johannesburg but her parents are from Wynberg and have been instructed to present me with the flowers.

The live election television coverage shows voter lines stretching across the country. Aerial photographs capture the curving lines cutting across every neighbourhood in rural villages and urban centers. Other than in KwaZulu-Natal, where fighting has continued sporadically between different local groups, I do not expect political difficulties. Logistical problems are to be expected. Stations opening late here and there and running out of ballot papers. Queues too long and unwieldy. But the predicted mayhem is not materialising. Those who had stocked up with candles, tinned food and who dug trenches in their back yards in anticipation of catastrophe must be sorely disappointed. I guess there will always be those who are able to see only the worst possibilities in life.

The tea, coffee and cakes are spread across the table. My brother Adam adds bottles of cooldrinks for the visitors who are in and out. This is one celebration that we think we all deserve. It is one that I would not have missed for anything. I have to go back to Johannesburg tonight to round off our election task.

Four months ago the Transitional Executive Council (TEC), our interim government, had appointed me to the Independent Media Commission (IMC) with six other media professionals. It was our job to oversee the relations between the media and political parties. We had to work out formulae to ensure fair coverage for the different parties and to mediate conflicts between the parties and media companies.

All of us working for the IMC as well as those working for the Independent Electoral Commission (IEC) were given permission to cast an early vote at our offices in central Johannesburg. I could not. Enjoying this historic moment with family, friends and neighbours was not something I was prepared to forego.

As I sip my tea in the chattering, warm kitchen, nibbling on a chocolate, I am Ivy Kriel as she nuzzles her nose into Ashley's shoulder. You did not die in vain, Ashley. You did not die in vain.

Two weeks later, I am at the Union Buildings in Pretoria. We are waiting for Madiba to arrive and deliver his inaugural address. I have brought my dad with me. He is wearing his famous red fez. He cannot sit still. Namane Magcau is sitting beside me, her arm locked through mine. A social science expert, she was one of the commissioners serving on the IMC with me. Her short hair is tightly cropped against her scalp. The brightness of her traditional pink dress with petals of blue, yellow and white embroidered around the neckline, across the chest and onto the sleeves matches her broad smile. We had been at each other's side through the difficult dramas of the past weeks. Old guard civil servants made all the files in my cabinet disappear. Curriculum vitae of personnel to be considered for employment somehow never got to us. A policeman posing as a civil servant was placed in charge of our finances. All sorts of strange inexplicable events unfolded, enmeshed in the tension between the old and the new. Without Namane's support, the strain would have been unbearable.

"I can see your dad can't wait for Madiba to arrive," she says.

"Well, we had to get up at 4 a.m. to be here on time, so I think the day is going to be rather long for him," I say.

"I can see he is very happy," she says.

"But let me help him with his boredom," I say.

I call him: "Dad, you see those cameras over there. They are going directly into people's televisions at home so that they can see what is going on here. Why don't you walk across those steps in front of them? If you do that your friends will all see you back home."

I do not have to tell him twice. He grins, turns around and walks directly across the path of the cameras, up and down.

Holding his right hand aloft, Madiba takes the oath of office: "In the presence of those assembled here and in full realisation of the high calling I assume as President in service of the Republic of South Africa, I do hereby swear to be faithful to the Republic of South Africa, and do solemnly and sincerely promise at all times to promote that which will advance and to oppose all that may harm the Republic: to obey, observe, uphold and maintain the Constitution and all other Law of the Republic; to discharge my duties with all my strength and talents to the best of my knowledge and ability and true to the dictates of my conscience; to do justice to all; and to devote myself to the well-being of the Republic and all its people."

Namane and I jump to our feet, joining South Africans of all colours and creeds and international guests as a thunderous applause welcomes the new president. Numerous ovations later, he stands at attention, silent, jaw set firm, serious. I hear a dull droning in the distance and then the planes whoosh past in coordinated formation to mark the moment. I am on my feet again. My dad is crying. On the podium in the line-up of dignitaries he points out his friend Sheikh Nazeem with his wife, Sabeega.

I laugh through my tears, happy for him. Before I can recover, three helicopters appear from behind the buildings. From each machine hangs the new South African flag, flapping in the morning air. I remember how awful we thought those colours and design were when they were first presented to us. Black, green and gold alongside red, white and blue.

Now a joyous roar affirming its beauty rises from the crowd. No. The roar comes not only from the crowd around me but from my own stomach, my chest, through my throat. Deep and gutteral elation filling the wide expansive blue sky, floating into infinity.

Back at my apartment in Johannesburg, I call my mother to share with her the joy of today. "So wonderful. So wonderful. We were glued to the television and what a treat it was to see your dad strutting across the screen. His friends have been calling all afternoon. They saw senior. It was hard for anybody who knows him to miss the fez," she says.

Proud as a peacock he was, as I am, as we all are, feathers interlocking, colours blending, merging, connecting, at last part of one whole.

Proud peacocks.

Chapter Seventeen

Mozena and I spread the white sheets over the floor so that they completely cover the carpet. We collect as many cushions as we can from Mansoor and Kayzuran's home and arrange these all along the wall so that guests will sit comfortably.

"Ruschka, fetch all our cushions next door," I say to her as she pops her head in at the door. She is dressed in a white thaub (long prayer dress) with her head swathed in a white scarf. She is a miniature version of me and Mozena.

I have invited female family and friends to a gadat (a special prayer session) to strengthen me for the year ahead. Usually, families ask special gadat groups to chant the rhythmic verses in a sing-song way. My father was not too happy but I had decided to invite just women both to curtail numbers and to allow maximum participation. I find that when the men are around, they take centre-stage with the women either preparing food in the kitchen or chatting in the bedrooms adjacent to the lounge.

In a week's time, I leave for New York to complete my masters degree in Journalism at Columbia University.

We are preparing the space for prayer in Mansoor's lounge because my lounge would barely seat twenty people on the floor and then I would have to take all the furniture out. Mansoor's lounge next door should comfortably seat about sixty guests, which will be adequate for tonight.

At the time of my divorce, my parents had moved from their home to a smaller house belonging to my sister, Julie. It had taken us a year of discussion to come to the decision about where they would live. Staying next to Julie was a good arrangement because both she and her husband were medical doctors and could be at hand to attend to any ailments. Now my brother Mansoor lived in my parents' house, and I lived in an apartment attached to it.

My parents had departed from the tradition that insists our elderly stay with their sons. My brothers had not been entirely happy about this departure from the convention, but over time they had accepted this to be a good arrangement. I had always admired my parents for being guided by Islamic law and tradition yet never hesitating to make entirely practical decisions informed by concrete daily reality. We have avoided a lot of pain in that way. Making rules stick when they are clearly not suitable for a particular situation can sometimes destroy perfectly harmonious relations. In addition to my parents' own willingness to bend the rules where appropriate, my father was quite obsessed with calling family gatherings to make collective decisions. Not that this approach always worked but it had its merits.

Often we were irritated because meetings took so much time and exposed us to all our different moods and temperaments, but it did teach us the art of accommodation, a particularly strong family feature.

Mozena is stirring the pot of boeber on the stove as relatives and friends begin to arrive. Boeber is a milk drink, with sago, cinnamon, cardamom, sugar and vermicelli. I like to cook it slowly just before we break our fast when the sweet scents pass up my nose into my brain, triggering a sense of ease in anticipation of the end of the day. My sister-in-law Razia carries in a box of cups and saucers and extra teaspoons that I have asked her to bring to serve the boeber.

"I am putting the trays and cups next door in my kitchen," I say to her. "It's going to be easier to leave everything there so that we can prepare the plates."

Razia is the one who takes over the supervision of the serving. We have learnt to accept her in this role that she loves and acquiesce when she is around. She tells us what to do and we do it. A very good system in a family where we all have different ideas about how things ought to be done. On the big festive days when the whole family gathers, we share the planning and making of the food but when it comes to the management of the dishing and serving, we leave it to Razia.

As the guests come, the cakes are flowing over the kitchen table onto the cupboard tops. It is the tradition that each guest brings a contribution to the evening. Ring doughnuts, koesisters, coconut tarts, jam tarts, cup cakes with icing sugar, snowballs, milk tart. All I had to do was buy some cardboard plates and some plastic clingwrap to give every guest a selection of cakes to take home with them.

When friends join our festivities, they always marvel at the amount and variety of foods we serve. What they often do not know is that what they see represents the collective contribution of all family members and friends.

This is an aspect of the strong Eastern influence which came across the seas three centuries ago when the Dutch colonised the Indonesian archipelego. They brought local men and women, often members of the elite considered to be trouble-makers, to work as slaves in the Dutch kitchens at the Cape. Some were held chained at night in dungeons at farming estates such as Groot Constantia, not far from where I live. Others were held in captivity on Robben Island where they died. Many provided the backbone of the artisan community that developed the Cape Colony.

The women slip off their shoes before stepping onto the expansive sheets and settle into comfortable nooks with their cushions as Yasmina Pandy and her friend prepare to start the prayers. Yasmina is a young activist well schooled in the Islamic tradition and lives in Wynberg. I have collected a number of kitābs (books) for everyone to share so that we can all follow and repeat the verses they are chanting. Slowly the lively verses develop into a steady beat thrumming through my body. I can feel the energy flowing into me as I drink from the sounds rising from the group. Some guests are dressed in the traditional thaub while others, like my mother, wear skirts covering their knees, cardigans and scarves draped around their heads pinned in different ways. My Christian, agnostic and atheist friends have come decked in colourful scarves blending easily into the floral, navy-blue, cream and black variety breaking the blandness of the white sheets. The dashes of colour reinforce the cheerful, warm ambience in the large room.

I cover my head with a scarf on special occasions. Generally I feel happier without one. I love the sense of fresh air against my scalp and the feel of the wind blowing through my hair. I refuse to display proof of my relationship with God through my dress. There is no such imposition on men. It's in fact nobody's business but my own. Only I can know what is in my heart. I can never know what is in the heart of another.

I am so happy that my mom is here tonight. She chooses not to squat down on the floor and finds a chair at the side of the room where she makes herself comfortable. As I look at her, I realise I have never seen her in public without a scarf. She is often bare-headed in the privacy of her home but outside it's different. That was how she was raised and that is what makes her most comfortable.

I remember the story about the one time when she did feel compelled to take off her scarf, loosen her hair, don a sun-hat and walk into the centre of the city. She was trying to disguise herself so that the security police would not recognise her as she lurked in the vicinity of the doctor's office. For days, different members of the family took turns to monitor the doorway to the office hoping that I would be taken to the doctor for a check-up. Twice they were rewarded. On the one occasion I saw my father and my sister-in-law Naiema on the pavement outside, and the next time I slipped a note to my sister-in-law Zerene, who managed to hop into the lift alongside me and my captors. The next day, she miscarried and everybody was convinced that the strain had been too great for her.

Tonight, all my sisters surround me except one. Julie is down with the flu. As I think of her, I make a mental note to diarise Junaid's birthday this year so that I will not forget to call her from New York.

At the end of about an hour, it is time for me to say a few words. I keep it short, emphasising how I feel that I am going to study further not only for my own benefit but for the benefit of everybody gathered here and the broader community. Gradually my personal needs are beginning to take priority, although I am unable to admit it. I will be living outside the country for a protracted period for the first time in my life and I am looking forward to the change.

After I have spoken the chattering starts, the food is brought in with many hands and the jokes follow. I sense that there is not complete approval that I am leaving my child behind to study abroad for nine months. I have arranged for her to join me after three months, to spend three months with me and then to come home while I complete the last three months. That is the plan.

Men very seldom have to consider their children when they are presented with such an opportunity. Women in their family do whatever they can to support them. In my case, the disapproval is not strong but I do sense it subtly. Fortunately I am blessed with a mother and sister who are prepared to help, without whom I know I can never do what I am doing.

"You girls must study," my mom used to say. "I want you to be independent and do the things I could never do. You must never forget the deen (religion) but you must study."

From the stories I have heard, both my grandmothers were women committed to education. My father's mother, Aisha Safodien, was a pre-school teacher. My mother's mother, Gadija Hendricks, was one of those accused of teaching her children the ways of the Christians.

"Wat makeer met Dieja?" said the community. "Haar kinders praat Engels en speel die klavier. Wil sy vir hulle kris maak?"(What's the matter with Gadija? Her children speak English and play the piano. Does she want to turn them into Christians?)

Two of my aunts were primary school teachers and one trained as a nurse. While none of the women on either side of the family had ever gone to university, my sister and I came from a tradition of educated women and we were proud of that fact. My mother, who had opted to marry when she was seventeen and had my three brothers by the time she was twenty-one, had not pursued further studies. Rearing her children has been her full-time profession. She was also an avid reader and we benefited from her intense relationship with the local library, watching her read before she slept every night and whenever she could snatch a spare moment during the day.

She must have been one of the last people of colour who persisted in keeping her membership of the Wynberg Library after they barred us, declaring it for whites only. As children, we moved to a small library opened above the fish-shop, close to the bus terminus on the Coloured side of Wynberg. My mother was furious and continued to visit the library classified white until she was asked to leave.

The guests are slowly saying their goodbyes. Ruschka and her young cousins run in and out of the kitchen where the cakes are being arranged. They carry the colourful plates covered in plastic to the lounge next door so that each guest has a selection of cakes to share with families at home.

After the last guests have left, Mozena and I sit briefly at the kitchen table to take a short break before doing the final tidying. Ruschka, in her white taub with her scarf hanging around her neck, comes through the door, takes one look at us and heads straight for the comfort of her other mother's large, comfortable lap.

A few days later, before I leave, Oom Gov arrives with his doctor, Mamisa Chabula. She is an unusual woman. Not only does she run the biggest medical practice in the township of Motherwell in Port Elizabeth, but she is also mother to ten children, five boys and five girls. Her afro hairstyle and gold-rimmed spectacles sit easily with a beige tailored jacket and brown pants. Although this is the first time we have met, we have had contact over the telephone for the years since his release and are delighted to have this opportunity to spend time together. Chauffeured by his friendly driver, who had the odd name of Cupid, the three of us glide into the city to attend a farewell symphony concert.

Oom Gov in his dark suit, white cuff-linked shirt and pinned tie, his head held high, strides into the City Hall and up its winding stairs with us on either side. His pleasure is palpable: not bad at all for an old man to be flanked by two younger women. His eyes have softened and he chuckles to himself. Conscious of the moment, Mamisa and I are both amused.

Enjoying Cape Town's Philharmonic Orchestra is a novel experience for me. As a child, my mom regularly attended performances on a Sunday afternoon. This became impossible for her in adulthood since all people of colour were denied access to this treat. Our lives were cut off from these influences. Since change has come, the orchestra's administrators are sensitive to the disparities and conscious of the need to broaden their audience. They are facing nearly fifty years of denied opportunities that require costly interventions.

We are seated in one of the small balconies that jut out above the rows of seats in the spacious, echoing hall. The chief violinist strokes his instrument. Waves of haunting notes ripple across the air, sending a thrill through my stomach. The conductor raises his baton, unleashing heavy baritone chords. Oom Gov nods his head slightly from side to side, moving his right hand in unison to the beat. For once, he does not drop off to sleep. My eyes remain on him and Mamisa as the concert ends. Good company is not always easy to come by. Yet I cannot deny that I am excited to leave behind my tightly-knit circle and once again venture into the unknown. Columbia University, here I come.

CHAPTER EIGHTEEN

Ruschka has come and gone and I am alone. I am on my way to B'nai Jeshuran, one of the oldest Jewish congregations in New York. I have done the rounds of the mosques and live right opposite St John the Divine, the biggest Anglican Cathedral in the USA. Often, I take my books and find a comfortable spot in the cathedral to savour the quietness. A seminar covering religion is taking me to a synagogue for the first time in my life.

My dad used to work for a Jewish family and I remember his stories. Jewish people were not supposed to work on a Saturday and had to walk everywhere and it was my dad's job to drop his boss around the corner from the synagogue, which in the strictest sense meant he wasn't driving and breaking the sabbath rules; but it also ensured that other congregants didn't see him in a car. My dad used to love telling this story, along with the story of the drunk who came into the shop to buy a steak-and-kidney pie. When the shopkeeper hands him the pie, he says: "Bhai, is die 'n halaal pie?" (Sir, is this a pie prepared according to Islamic rules?) He was always careful not to joke about any other religion without poking fun at his own.

As I walk down 110th Street, where I live, to the underground, I am momentarily transported back a few weeks to when my sister Julie arrived with Ruschka and a group of her cousins.

I have to fetch them at Grand Central station. They have taken the train from Washington, where they have been visiting my brother-in-law's relatives. There are seven of them with suitcases. How am I going to get them from Grand Central to 110th Street? We all struggle down the long flights of steps onto the local line. One look at the bags and the crowds and I realise that we will never all be able to get onto the train before the doors click closed. I have no option but to ask some of the commuters to give us a hand.

"Would you help us lift these bags on and off the train when it comes," I ask a tall blond man in a black overcoat. He smiles broadly and is most obliging, as are a few other commuters. Once inside the train, we stand bunched up, squashed by these huge bags. I just have to say it: "This is my family and they are not moving to New York. They are just visiting."

The people around us laugh. "Mummy," Ruschka is tugging at my arm. She whispers. "Mummy, please don't talk to the people."

My poor child. I am embarrassing her. She just wants to blend into the crowd. "Rusch, we need help here and I have to ask."

It's March and the icy weather has subsided. I smile, deeply sunk in the memory of that visit, thinking of the days when we were holed up in our apartment in the middle of the blizzard of '96. It was the one and only time that I had seen the busy streets of New York shut down completely. As luck would have it, my family was visiting at the same time that Mary Kay's son and his friend arrived.

When I had first met Mary Kay Blakely, with whom I was going to have to share an apartment, five months previously, I had looked at her through my prejudiced South African eyes. Her blue eyes, her grey hair and her agitated temperament had fitted my preconception of an American person. The accommodation arranged involved us sharing, however, and I knew I would just have to make do for the nine months that I was here.

With time, our paths had crossed in the narrow kitchen we shared and had become firmly intertwined. I learnt about her world and she about mine and slowly the blinkers were removed.

Ruschka had loved it when we found ourselves trapped in the apartment for two days with all the world a white wonder outside.

Despite this, I could not convince her to stay with me for three months. At age nine, she was perceptive and could see that this isolated living in an apartment in a huge city would not be the best for her.

As I jump aboard the train, having reached the station where my family had finally disembarked with their fourteen suitcases, I try and blot out the memory of Ruschka screaming as we said goodbye at the airport. She wanted to go but did not want to leave me behind. Julie was kind enough to telephone me from the departure lounge two hours later to assure me that she had stopped screaming. It reminded me of those early days when I used to leave her at the pre-school in Wynberg.

Anyway, it probably all happened for the best. It would have been tough for me to complete this programme and at the same time see to the needs of a nine-year-old.

The course is not quite what I had expected. I had hoped to be at a university where I could reflect, read and deepen my understanding of the challenges facing my profession. The school was, however, organised like a boot camp, training journalists to be ready for the pressures of the media environments they would find themselves in once they graduated. They did not train the journalists to think beyond the drill, beyond the basic formulae of how to present a story. Perhaps some were lucky enough later to find their own paths. Most were left in a straightjacket without a critical understanding of the different ways to view the world.

Waiting at the entrance of the synagogue are a number of my fellow students. We enter and seat ourselves on the wooden prayer benches.

New York has the largest Jewish community in the world – larger than any city in Israel. Over three million Jewish people live here.

Today, congregants are gathered for the annual Purim festivities, which celebrate the Jewish triumph against Prime Minister Haman, who served the king of Persia five centuries before Christ. A member of the congregation starts reading the scroll of Esther in Hebrew. Each time the name "Haman" is mentioned, the synagogue fills with a cacophony of rattles. Children and their parents stomp their feet, boo and swing their rattles, which are like the ones we buy in Adderley Street on New Year's Eve. They make a loud crackling sound. The reader pauses, smiles and allows the parents and their children the time to share in the affirmation of triumph against wrong.

The little girls are dressed in golden dresses with crowns on their heads. Numerous Queen Esthers crowd together at the front of the synagogue as two rabbis with prayer shawls over their shoulders twirl their right hands in the air to encourage them to swing their rattles at the appropriate moment. It is a prayer service that looks more like a school concert. A few parents wear tall, brightly-coloured hats, sharing the moment with their children. Together they sing the song prepared by the congregation's performing group: "Imagine there's no evil . . ." to the tune of John Lennon's "Imagine".

Their voices carry my thoughts to the difficult issues facing us back home. The Truth and Reconciliation Commission has been created in my absence. Activists are debating whether they should testify or not. When I go home in a few months' time, I will have to decide whether I will participate in the process. But sitting here in this synagogue, I am particularly concerned about how we will keep alive the memory of the wrongs committed against millions in our country. How will we remember without seeking vengeance? How are we to forgive when the pain is so intense and the memory so fresh? What do we do so that our children and theirs may never again be subjected to the same humiliation of our generation?

These children and their parents hold rattles in their hand to break the silence against injustice. How are we to ensure that our children too will shout together with us when the word "apartheid" is mentioned?

The congregants hug one another at the end of the service. They have brought to memory an event that occurred five centuries before Christ. I wonder if any of them link these principles of justice and triumph to the situation presently facing people in the Middle East. Does anyone in this congregation have any idea of the hardships facing the Palestinians? I look around but am not sure who to ask. I have come here to observe this ritual to satisfy the school's requirement, just as I have visited local churches and mosques. Let me not complicate everybody's life by asking the uncomfortable questions. For once, let me just get up here, register an interesting experience and go home to my lovely friend Mary Kay who is preparing my favourite potato and leek soup for supper.

At home, I collect a letter from the postbox. It's from South Africa and I cannot wait to open it. I can smell the soup simmering on the gas stove and hear Mary Kay's voice calling out her usual welcome from behind her room door: "Hi, sweetie. Be out in a minute."

I tear open the envelope and slip the cream paper onto my bed. The letterhead reads: Parliament of the Republic of South Africa. Following in small print are the words: Deputy President of the Senate.

Dear Beida
It was wonderful hearing from you as per your very short postcard. Thanks for the address and hope that you are not shifting about as I understand they do in New York from week to week . . .

I feel connected to Oom Gov through history and our interest in journalism. I value his comments on my writing and he values mine. And of course we share, too, a love of music.

His characteristic chuckle fills my mind as I read and am reminded of what a great tease he is.

How are you and how is the fast tempo of New York treating you? Hope you have not yet found kindhearted gentlemen in New York to make your heart and head turn in circles. It is good to keep a cool head in a world that offers little stability to say nothing of a straight, be it narrow path.

He was not teasing, though, when I saw him days before I left for New York. He was quite the stern grandfather, warning me about unsavoury suitors in foreign cities. He has obviously not forgotten and has felt it necessary to remind me. But I have to laugh when he asks for advice, notwithstanding his lofty admonitions.

I have been getting invitations from all the orchestral concerts but who was I going to go along with! Have you any suggestions? Incidentally I have received a letter from the Director-General of the Cape Town Symphony Orchestra inviting me to be their Patron-in-Chief – I am accepting . . .

I visualize his right hand with fingers curled, moving from side to side to the beat of Mozart's Symphony No. 40 in G Minor as his head moves in unison.

He must have dictated the letter to his secretary, Sheila, who has neatly typed it out, allowing him to scribble his scrawling signature at the end.

The very best of wishes.
Love
Oom Gov

An old-fashioned letter through the post beats e-mail any day. It can be held, touched and smelt. I place it carefully with my mom's precious letters on the pedestal beside my bed. Together they remind me of the strong link that binds me to a country far far away at the tip of the African continent where I belong.

CHAPTER NINETEEN

I walk into the press gallery to listen to the finance minister, Trevor Manuel, deliver his annual budget address. This morning, I held our country's budget in my hands for the first time. I am political editor of the *Daily News* and covering parliament, a position long denied to all journalists of colour. Women of colour were especially suspect.

The minister is immaculately dressed in a dark suit, a white shirt and a red tie.

He looks very different from Trevor the activist I remember dressed in a leather jacket astride his motorbike. My mother called me in New York on the day Madiba announced that he would be our new finance minister. I wrote to him immediately, posting the letter to my mom. I was very proud of him and asked him please to forget his penchant for women now that he was holding such a key position. It was not so much out of concern for his morality that I did it – more that I dreaded the thought of being the journalist asked to cover his indiscretions.

Today he is delivering his maiden speech. In the visitors gallery, next to us, sits his wife, Lynn Mathews, a dedicated activist in her own right, their three sons, Govan, Pallo and Jamie. Next to them is his mother, Philma Manuel. I could never have imagined Philma, a clothing worker and single parent, sitting on a seat in the gallery so long reserved for whites. Philma who worked hard in the factory so that Trevor could further his studies at the Peninsula Technikon, the college designated for Coloureds under apartheid.

Ruschka is agitated when I get home. She has become a rather clingy ten-year-old. She had pined for me when I was in New York and I am having to pay the price. She is not interested in watching Uncle Trevor on the television news.

"Come and see. Perhaps you will see Govan," I say. Trevor's son and she were at pre-school together. I cannot get through to her. She does not want me to go out at night. She does not want to stay with a baby-sitter. I have finally figured it out that she is terribly threatened by her father's new relationship.

I decide that tonight's the night we will sit down for a chat after supper.

"Ruschie, it's normal for your dad to have another woman in his life. You need to accept this and not be so angry."

"He does not love me anymore, mom," she says.

"He does, sweetie pie. He will always love you."

She is not convinced. I thought the chat would ease her but she appears even more tense. I can see that there's nothing to be gained from pushing the point. When she tumbles into her bed, I reach for the bottle of calming oil in the bathroom cupboard, sit at the foot of her bed and pour oil onto my hands so that I can rub her feet. She loves it and the tense expression fades as she falls asleep.

Weeks later I am desperate enough to go for advice to the Parents Centre in Claremont. Ruschka remains in a sombre, angry state. After listening to me, the director, Fawzia Rykliff, puts her finger on the problem.

"You are telling her to forgive her father and to accept his life. But she is angry. Very angry. The more you are telling her to forgive and understand, the angrier she is becoming."

I am astounded. I thought I was giving her the best guidance a parent could give by not breaking down her relationship with her father in any way.

"What must I do?" I ask sheepishly.

"You need to tell her that you respect her right to be angry. That she has a right to be angry and that while you have accepted her father's new life, you cannot force this onto her. That it is up to her if she wants to forgive him for whatever he did that upset her."

This is something I had not considered. It is worth a try. It turns out to be invaluable advice. Although she is still angry, the anxiety between us fall away immediately and her natural brightness is slowly making its way back into our lives.

"Mom, why can't I come with you?" says Ruschka.

"It's better if you go to school today."

"But why? Riaad is going to be there."

"Riaad is nineteen years old, you are only ten, sweetie. I am going to speak about all the awful things that happened long ago and I think you are too young to listen to all of that."

She purses her lips, her round cheeks tighten as she clenches her teeth, showing her disappointment. She has inherited that habit from her dad. Still, she is not one to make a fuss. She goes to the kitchen to fetch her sandwiches from the refrigerator and packs them into her schoolbag.

It's hard for me to explain to her that I am very unsure about what lies ahead today. Last night, I called Julie and confessed that I was finding it very difficult to go through with the testimony. The organisers of the Truth and Reconciliation Commission had asked if I would testify at a special hearing focussing on women to mark our national women's day. I had agreed but yesterday I had been gripped by feelings of anxiety and panic.

"I don't want to talk about these things," I said to her. "I have blocked them out of my memory and when I try and recall, I feel like I am falling to pieces. I am not going to be able to cope."

"Do you want to do this?" she asks.

"Yes and no."

Yes, because I believe that this cathartic process allows me the opportunity to bring closure to an ugly phase of my life. No, because I am very scared that I will not be able to hold on to the rather fragile calm facade that successfully gets me through my daily chores.

The process of blocking off feeling had started that first night in the cells of Milnerton police station in 1980. My mind could only cope with thoughts of the beautiful sea rolling on to the beach, a kilometre away from where I was being held. In my mind's eye, I fixated on the sea with Table Mountain in the background, blotting out the terror gripping my soul.

Julie suggested that I put a small calming tablet under my tongue before I speak, in the hope that it will help me cope.

This morning, my emotions are no more consistent. I feel I want to testify but I also don't want to. I particularly don't want Ruschka to be weighed down by the detail of the torture at such a young age.

I arrive at the main hall at the University of the Western Cape where the special hearings are to take place.

As I step into the lobby adjacent to the hall, I hear somebody calling me.

"Ms Jaffer!" I turn towards the pleasure-filled voice and there is Elizabeth Erasmus, now Cloete, walking towards me.

Seeing her dark face and braided hair makes me smile and remember that day ten years ago when she, accused of sewing thousands of ANC flags, defiantly attached black, green and gold beads to the ends of her braids.

"Elizabeth, my dear!" We hug. "Why are you here today?" I ask.

"Don't you know that I work for the TRC?"

"Yes, I know that but I am not sure what it is you are doing."

"It is my job to see to the logistics of the hearings, that we have a venue, enough chairs, that all recording equipment works, you know, that sort of thing."

Long gone are her days of sitting in front of a sewing machine at a factory in Epping, straining her back to push garments passed from one worker to another under her needle.

"I am so glad that you are here today," I say. She smiles and ushers me into the hall to take my seat alongside seven other women who have come to testify.

Pain is universal yet so particular, Albie once said. We all have our own ways of dealing with pain. It's not something that can be legislated into uniformity. Often foreigners expect pat answers to questions of reconciliation and forgiveness in our country but I know there can never be a single solution following a single formula. There are those who marvel at Madiba's ability to forgive and quote his stance as the ideal, but then, on close examination, we know that he too is conflicted. He is able to have tea with Betsy Verwoerd, the wife of one of the prime architects of apartheid, but cannot reconcile with Winnie, his wife and long-time companion. Human emotions are complex and cannot be slotted into neat little boxes. Each of our journeys is unique, similar yet so dissimilar. Any notion that someone somewhere out there in the world will be able to take away the pain lodged within our spirits is mistaken. We each have to trudge our own path through that pain and I am so aware that this is what I have to do this morning.

Seated on the stage at the front of the UWC hall is advocate Denzil Potgieter, dressed in a dark suit, white shirt and carefully knotted dark tie. He is the only man on today's panel. Archbishop Tutu has handed over the chairing duties to commissioner Glenda Wildschut in an attempt to further emphasise the central position of women in today's proceedings. She is on Denzil's left. Next to her are commissioners Mary Burton and Wendy Orr. They are seated at two long tables covered with white cloths. Microphones on stands are spread along the tables and on each table, somebody has placed a jug of water and a few drinking glasses. Behind the table, pinned to the long dark curtains, stretches a big TRC banner. On the side of the banner, next to one table, stands a flagpole holding high the new South African flag. It provides the finishing touch, adding the necessary formality to the setting.

After a short prayer, Denzil asks two women, Nomfundo Walaso and Cheryl de la Rey, to introduce the special women's hearings.

I am too nervous to clearly hear what they are saying. I dig in my bag for the little plastic packet with the small pill my sister slipped to me earlier. I grip the tiny pill between my thumb and forefinger, then place it under my tongue. I vaguely hear the women tell the history of our national women's day.

On 9 August, 1956, tens of thousands of women gathered outside the Union Buildings in Pretoria to protest against women also having to carry the hated pass imposed upon their men. Their powerful message to the then Prime Minister Strijdom was if you strike a woman, you strike a rock and will be crushed. The magnitude of the protest forced the authorities to reconsider their policy. They withdrew the decision to make women carry passes . . .

I close my eyes and pray. "Dear God, give me the strength to see this through. Please give me the strength to see this through."

Eventually, I am up on the stage, part of me prepared to speak, another part wanting to flee as far away as possible. My tongue feels heavy. Had the pill been too strong? How on earth am I going to speak?

Glenda senses my hesitation. "We know it is not easy for you to tell your story at such a public forum but there are many people out there who are supportive of you today and we hope we will afford you the opportunity as the TRC to listen very carefully and attentively to what you have to tell us."

How do I tell her what I feel when I cannot feel anything? I have to start somewhere.

"Thank you very much for giving me this opportunity to speak," I say. "I am very aware that this is just one little story amongst so many others. So if I tell the story, I am telling it to illustrate what has happened to so many other women."

I am deeply conflicted about this focus on my personal history. There is a tussle between a part of me that says each person is entitled to affirm their own history and another part that is intensely conscious of being just one little speck in a bigger scheme of things.

Where did it all begin? In 1966, at age eight, when Dimitri Stafendas stabbed Prime Minister Hendrik Verwoerd to death and we cringed in our classroom as police vans flew past our school? In 1967, at age nine, when my father kept me from school because the principal at Douglas Road Primary School had decided to comply with a departmental instruction to hoist the apartheid flag and make us sing the national anthem? In 1969, at age eleven, when Imām Abdullah Haroon was killed in detention? In 1973, at age fifteen, when one of my dedicated teachers belonging to the Unity Movement invited me to secret meetings to discuss opposition to apartheid? In 1976, at age eighteen, when I watched my friend Tony Cochrane brutally

127

beaten by the riot police on the parade opposite Cape Town's railway station? Or was it that same day, when a doctor at UCT where we were both students refused to treat him, leaving me to get him back home by train, suffering from serious concussion? Was it at the end of 1979 when I observed trade unionists Virginia Engel and Oscar Mphetha lead the Fattis and Monis workers to victory in one of the Cape's most memorable strikes?

For the purposes of the TRC, I start the story a year later in 1980, when I was twenty-two years old.

I tell of how I wrote the story that changed my life. How the police would not give the *Cape Times* the detail of who they had killed and how my editor, Tony Heard, had asked me to track down the families.

I seem to be rambling on and on in a monotonous way. I cannot hear myself easily. It seems so distant.

God, I am only at the beginning of this story. Would I not be taking up too much time? I pause. But I cannot stop now. The commissioners see me pause and quickly one of the staff brings me a glass of water.

I start again and can hear what I am saying. A few days after the story was published I was detained.

"They came to my house early in the morning. My dad woke me up. I had just come from night shift at two. They picked me up at five, giving no reasons for my detention. They simply stated they wanted to take me off for a week. When I asked where they were taking me, whether they were taking me to Pollsmoor Prison, Spyker, the notorious Spyker, said to me as we were going out of my mom's house, he said Pollsmoor Prison is a five-star hotel compared to where you are going. And then he threatened that they were going to break my nose and beat me up and that was as I walked out of the house, out of my parents' house."

I am stuttering and my neck constricts. It feels as if a leather belt is being tightened around my throat. The bright lights of the television cameras are now turned onto me and I see only a blur of faces looking up at me from the audience below. I cannot see my sister, her son, my brother, my mother and father.

"I had absolutely no idea what was going to happen to me."

Day in and day out the interrogation went on, I tell the commission. Then they stopped and offered me some hot food.

Silently my mind races ahead as I speak. How could I have known that they had drugged the food. It was a version of the drug doctors give alcoholics to make them violently sick if they dare take any alcohol. That's what the doctor told me who had examined me after my release.

I feel numb and my mouth is dry but I remember.

"Give us a name of any person you know who belongs to the ANC. Any name. Just one name. Tell us!" says the hairy-handed, tall captain with the steely blue eyes, the man of my nightmares.

At a certain point I start stretching my mind to come up with one possible name. I am beyond hysteria. We are in an interrogation room on the 6th Floor of the Sanlam Centre in Port Elizabeth. He takes me to the window and says he will throw me down there because that's where they kill people. He takes me into an adjacent office where there is a telephone. He leaves me standing in the middle of the larger room and makes a call to somebody. I hear them talking about my writing, about my reporting. They talk about the interviews with the victims of the police shootings in Elsies River and Lavender Hill. A shortened version of the full-page story had appeared in the *Eastern Province Herald*. It has the captain raving.

He ends his conversation abruptly and with his heavy hairy hand hits me across the room into the wall.

Shuddering. Shaking. Trembling. Four days and it has not stopped. Hollow eyes set deep in grey, deadened skin. Dandruff-covered hair. I look like a ghost when I see myself in the toilet mirror.

"Why would the police want to kill anyone if they were innocent?" they ask. "These were gangsters. They were thieves. They were robbers. It was all lies that you wrote about."

He turns as he hears somebody enter the room. It is a black security cop. He moves away from me and says to the man: "Just rape her, rape her."

He steps towards me as if he is going to follow the instruction and I feel as if I am about to die. And then he calls him away and says, leave her alone. They obviously are trying to get me completely to a point where I cannot function any more. The tragedy of it is that I didn't really have the information that would have satisfied them. I must say that I understand how people give information in a situation like that, because I did my best to think what I could possibly tell them.

I am losing my concentration. I feel it. I hear myself at a distance again. I am no longer aware of the audience. "Then he left and he left me in this room – left me in this room with these two policeman and he said to them he said to me – he said to them they must watch me. And they made me stand in the middle of the room and I just had to stand there and then at some point they allowed me to sit."

God, I am only at the first detention in 1980. How on earth am I going to describe ten years of ongoing harassment? I cannot stop now.

The men turn a fan onto me to prevent me from closing my eyes. Every time I nod off, they shout: "Maak jou oë oop." (Open your eyes.)

I am disappearing somewhere. I am not in the hall, nor am I in the interrogation room. I am disassociating. There are two me's – one me talking, another me hiding somewhere far, far away. The one me is saying: "And I started seeing – I started seeing all my veins in my hand dilating. And my arms, my veins in my hands and my arms and I . . . I felt pains across my chest and suddenly I started feeling like . . . all my insides were going to come out . . . And I said to them I am going to get sick, I am going to get sick . . ." And the one guy ran with me to the toilet and the other guy ran to the phone and he said: 'It's starting.' Now at that point I didn't think anything of it. I was just seeing all my veins dilating, it looked like worms – it looked like worms coming out of my hands.

"I thought my blood vessels were going to burst and I just felt these pains across my chest. Then Captain Du Plessis came back – the one who had been hung upside down from a tree in East Africa – and he said: 'Zubeida, you know, you are never going to make it, you're going to have a heart attack, you're going to die.'"

The turning point did not come that night. I slowly lost consciousness and by the next morning I am lying on the floor as the men observe me. At times I am aware that they are coming in and out of the room. They have thrust a pen and paper into my hands, but I am beyond being able to write. On Saturday afternoon, I am helped up, placed in a car and in a zombie-like state driven to Humansdorp, a town about an hour away from Port Elizabeth. There my body hits the thin felt mat in the cell, surfacing into consciousness only the next day.

I will never forget how they finally wrung answers from me, answers that were mine and not theirs to take. Unwelcome dentists moving with stealth in the cover of darkness.

Dragged from my Humansdorp cell in the middle of the night, standing, always standing, in a small room in the Sanlam Centre, the turning point had come, days after the tea and curry episode, after hours of interrogation standing on legs that were turning to jelly.

A Captain Oosthuizen from Grahamstown has joined the team. He wants to know the name of a journalist at the *Cape Times* who had written a story on the military. I say nothing.

"We want you to sign this statement," says Captain Oosthuizen. "We have prepared it for you to sign."

They give it to me. I cannot read it. It's all a blur. I am so terrified, fearing the endless interrogation and beating will start again. Fearing that they will kill me, as they have killed others in detention.

Remembering where I am, I offer a further explanation to the commissioners: "I've gone through newspaper cuttings now and I see that it says in the statement that I had been shown some ANC literature by Ian Ngijima, one of the students at Rhodes University where I was studying."

Back to the interrogation room. "We want your books, Zubeida. We did not find any of your books when we searched your house. Where are your books?" says the captain.

Tring-tring, tring-tring. The captain lifts the receiver, listens and then asks the caller to hold on. The telephone is in an office where I am being interrogated. It is my father on the line. They have taken my father. They have picked him up from his business in Grassy Park and taken him to Caledon Square. My throat constricts. I have difficulty in speaking.

"We have your father. Tell him where your books are. We want your books. Tell him or we will lock him up."

"Dad, where are you?"

" At Caledon Square, Beida."

My father was so soft, so sweet, so gentle. He had cried on the station when I left to study in Grahamstown. He had cried in front of all my friends, in front of strangers on the station. I told them whatever I could and lost my self-respect in the process.

I was released after forty-two days in detention and charged with possession of three banned books, the one being Franz Fanon's *Wretched of the Earth*.

I went on trial, was acquitted, and as I stepped down from the dock through the side door leading to the corridor, Spyker and his henchmen were there to block the way. In his hand he held a subpoena requiring me to testify as a state witness against Guy Berger, who was on trial in the Eastern Cape and had been my tutor at Rhodes University. He also had a train ticket ready for the next day so that I could leave for Port Elizabeth. I refused to take the documents and walked away. He had no option but to deal with my lawyers.

I don't tell the commission this, but a few days later, Trevor arrived and wandered with me into the yard. He had come with a plan to get me out of the country the next day. What was the point of facing a jail sentence and wasting my life in prison when I could be of help to the movement? He would come by in the morning to hear what I had decided and we would have to leave at once because all arrangements had been made.

What a long lonely night that was. I could not discuss this with anybody. I had been sworn to secrecy. Should I? Should I not? Should I? Should I not?

When he came the next morning I had decided. I would stay. I had heard stories about how people battled in exile, longing for home and their community.

"Trevor, I think I am going to waste more time going into exile than sitting in prison for a year," I said. "At least when I come out of prison, I come back to my family and community and all the people who make me feel safe and protected. In Swaziland or Zambia, it's going to take me longer than a year just to get used to new people and a new situation and at the end of that, I may not be able to come home for a long time. I will stay."

Trevor accepted my decision but I could see he was worried.

A week later, Guy changed his plea to guilty. In so doing, he saved fifty students, who had been called as witnesses, the trauma of having to decide whether they would testify or not. He was jailed for four years. I could go back to work.

But it was never quite the same again. I had great difficulty in concentrating. When I got off the train some mornings, the cops would be following me to work. A few months later, in May 1981, when I reported on the anti-Republic Day protests at UWC, my passport was withdrawn without explanation. A wild river had swept me from the safety of the shores and was twirling me around in its cross-currents.

There is so much to tell. I am conscious of the fact that eight of us are set down to testify today. I am allowed to speak for as long as I want to but I know that I have to strip years of intense experience down to its bare minimum.

I wish I could leave this place. It's just too much. But I have to go on. I need to explain about my second detention which in a strange sort of way I think I deserved. By then I was an activist and knew what was in store for me. But it was less painful, less terrifying, even, because at least I knew what I was there for. I had consciously decided to commit myself to a cause that I knew was dangerous. I accepted the consequences.

I start the story of the second detention but am short on detail. The procedure was the same as the first but the shock different. There was none of the acute terror and panic I had felt the first time, only a coldness and a calculated determination, so strong that it had brought my daily morning sickness to an abrupt end. I remember that I was painfully conscious that if I were sick, I would have to retch in view of the police woman posted at the door to watch me day and night. Even less did I want to be in that position were any of my interrogators to walk in. It would be demeaning, lessening my control over the situation and I was determined this time not to let that happen. The whole point was to make you lose control so that you could give information about yourself and your comrades that you would regret for the rest of your life.

The bed with its sheets and clean blankets was in a white cell at Sea Point Police Station – by 1985, they had become very cautious with Section 29 detainees. I was definitely enjoying the privileges that comrades had fought for and died for in police cells all over the country – how much pain and sadness did so many people suffer for this cell to be clean and this bed to be my sleeping place. These privileges had, of course, been the right of white criminals for decades.

My family had sent me an Arabic-English Qur'ān. It was my only reading material and my only companion through many lonely hours. The only way I could think of to survive was to tell myself that I had the task of reading the Qur'ān from cover to cover, in Arabic and in English. When I was finished with this task, I would be released. My days were full – sleep, exercise, showering in the courtyard when it was opened for half-an-hour in the morning and half-an-hour in the afternoon. Reading, pacing, singing . . . interrogation. At some point I stop, no longer able to go beyond the story of the threats to my unborn baby. There is some noise in the hall.

"I am sorry, Zubeida," says Glenda, "Carry on please."

"No," I say. "I don't think I want to say anything further." I am feeling completely numb. I know there is more to say but I have had enough. I just don't have the strength.

"Thank you for telling us your story," says Glenda. "I wonder if you will allow us to ask a few questions of clarification?"

I nod.

What's been the effect on your health? How did you know that you were drugged? Tell us more about Spyker van Wyk? You seem to suggest that he was polite in his manner? Did you ever see a doctor?

Glenda has the first question. Then Wendy Orr steps in. Then Mary Burton.

The questions are for all of us, for the people, for the country. But one of the questions, I think, is directly important to these women. "May I ask you why it is that you came before the commission today and what it is you would like us to respond to in your story?"

I realise this is very controversial because there were activists who had refused to come to the TRC. My own ex-husband had decided against it. He said we should bring a case against Mostert and let him face prosecution. The best I could do was to offer to help in whatever way I could if he chose to go that route. I wanted to be part of this process because I believed we had far more of a chance to publicise a wide range of injustices this way than we would have if we had to find the resources to bring everybody to trial. I also wanted to carry on with my life and the TRC process seemed to be providing me with the opportunity to symbolically break with the past.

I have to affirm that to the commission.

"I felt that I don't want to go into the future, into the years to come, and pass all this pain on to my daughter and future generations," I say.

"And as far as what I would like the commission to do, I mean I feel very strongly that these people who did these things should not be allowed to get away with it . . . they cannot possibly still hold these positions of authority. We need to know where they are.

" . . . I feel that they shouldn't be allowed to get away with it.

"They should be confronted, and they should be demoted at the very least. I am sure that many feel more should be done to them, but at least they should know that what they did was not right. We don't want them . . ."

I stop as I hear the strong clapping. I vaguely see the audience now. I still cannot make out too many faces but then I see my dad in his red fez and my mom next to him. My brother Yusuf, my dearest sister, Julie, and her son, Riaad.

"Thank you very much, Zubeida. Thank you very much for coming," says Glenda.

As I leave the stage, my limbs seem to creak like an old chair. My head feels dull.

I regret having ended so abruptly. I needed to complete the story of the second detention. For the sake of all who were listening but mainly for my own sake.

I remember a few days after Mostert had left the cell empty-handed, with no answers to record on his portable tape-recorder, I recited the last verse of the Qur'ān in Arabic and read its English translation. My task was done. There was no reason for me to continue being in this cell. This was the logic that had kept me sane as the days had passed into weeks.

I packed the few personal belongings I had into the small suitcase, unrolled a long piece of toilet paper, broke it off and used it to clean the cement bench on which the suitcase rested.

I wanted to be ready to leave immediately when they came to tell me I was going home.

The dark shadows were falling across the cell. It would soon be night and they had not come. All of the next morning, I waited expectantly to hear that familiar clang, clang of the keys in the courtyard door beyond the cell.

When that night came, I spoke with myself. Having nobody to speak to, I often spoke with myself.

"You must forget about being released," I said. "This is the worst thing you can do to yourself. You know it's the worst thing. When one is in prison, you must not think you are coming out. You must think you are going to be there a long time." That's what my lawyer, Dullah Omar, had said to me the last time.

I wanted so much to convince myself but it was hard. I had told myself for all these weeks that when I had completed reading the Qur'ān, I would be released. Now I had to find some other way of coping but was refusing to accept this.

It was easier the next morning. The day was bright. I could smell the salt sea air drifting through the grated windows. A certain calmness came over me but I still could not shake off the expectation of being released.

I dressed carefully, putting on my least-creased white and black dress, brushed out my long, heavy black hair, then covered my head with a green floral scarf.

The jangle of the key in the distance. Its metallic click in the lock. Then suddenly she stood in the doorway of the cell, smiling brightly, blue eyes sparkling, genuinely happy.

"I have come to take you home. You are going home," she said.

135

She stepped into the cell. "Come, you must pack your things."

"My things are packed," I said, knowing that all I needed to do now was zip up the suitcase.

Her face glowed. Sergeant Blom, trained as a primary school teacher, had tried in her own way to be kind to me. There was the ten rand she slipped to me from my mom when Mostert refused to take the fruit my mother had brought for me. She was a single parent with one small son – uncertain about her future.

"If the ANC comes here, then they are going to chop off our heads," she had said to me one day.

But then here I was representing the ANC, just a woman with all the needs that she had. Her kind, naturally good human instincts prevailed in her relations with me, blocking out completely her darker side.

Tall, blonde, blue eyes, Afrikaans-speaking with a reasonably good working knowledge of English. She chattered all the time as she led me from the cell to her car parked in the alleyway separating the police office from the cells in the yard.

Not even Mostert's efforts to restart the interrogation sessions when we arrived at the headquarters dampened her spirits. I just ignored him. I kept on looking up into her smiling, delighted face, watching it transform into a Cheshire cat when Mostert eventually agreed she could take me home instead of calling my family to collect me.

Her enthusiasm puzzled me. She seemed to be more delighted about my going home than I was at that point. I was still on my guard, expecting anything. What on earth was going on?

When her car stopped outside my mom's home it was about midday and I turned to say goodbye to her. "I hope you will think about what I have told you and leave this awful job you are doing," I said.

"I can't. What will I do?" she said.

"If you know what you are doing is wrong, you will find something else to do," I said.

My hand lifted the handle on the door and as it swung open, she asked: "Can I go in with you? I would like to very much."

God. Is this woman crazy? She is expecting me to go home with my jailer. I nodded, not knowing what else to say.

She followed me into the house. Two brothers in the kitchen with my mother. Eyes as huge as saucers.

"Beida!"

"Mom, it's Beida."

Shrieks of delight. Hugs. Tears. Words stumbling over words over shrieks, over tears. Mom. Mansoor and Adam.

I had forgotten about Blom until my mother noticed her. She was startled but then the family politeness kicked in. She offered Blom a seat and asked if she would like something to drink.

My shoulders tensed up as I watched her chatting to my mom and slowly lifting the glass of coke to her lips. The tension passed and, leaving them together, I joined my brother Adam in the sun-filled kitchen, feeling his strong arms around me, pulling me beyond those weeks of darkness that had cast a shadow over my soul.

CHAPTER TWENTY

Ruschka huddles beside me in the bed. It is a cloudy morning and I decide to lie in for a bit. Today is going to be a long day and I do not want to rush.

It is 10 May 2000, exactly six years after the inauguration of Mandela. President Mbeki is making a rare appearance to answer questions in the National Assembly this afternoon and I know that the chances of getting home early are slim. Four months after I started covering parliament, the company offered me the job of group parliamentary editor. It was not something I particularly wanted to do but I have been doing it for the past three years. Relaxed next to my child, I suddenly, unaccountably, have an unbidden and unpleasant flashback to the day I was appointed.

I am the only woman in a sea of unfriendly male faces. Not one of the men who now have to report to me extends a friendly hand of congratulations. The knowledge that my colleagues, Pippa and Alide, have invited me for lunch to celebrate is the only comfort. At least I have somewhere to describe the stifling experience.

Back from lunch I am confronted by Clive, one of the correspondents on the team. He is furious. His blue eyes are cold in his pale face. He glares at me.

"What do you think the company is going to do with you when you fail?" he says. "Where will you go?"

I am completely startled. I have never been confronted with such hostility from a colleague. From the state, yes. The police, yes. But a colleague?

I am quiet at first.

"What will you do?" he says again. "Where will you go?"

Deep inside me something stirs. I look at him and say very quietly. "It is possible for me to fail and I will face that when it comes. Anybody can fail."

Then my voice amplifies naturally. "I just want to tell you, however, that I haven't failed at anything I have done so far. I do not expect to fail at this."

I turn to Ruschka. "Your oupa is very sick, Rusch," I say. "If he is going to suffer like this, then I hope Allah will take him away." Her eyes mist over.

But I am in control. I feel I have accepted that my father will be leaving us soon. He fainted yesterday. My mom rushed to the intercom which links her home to my sister's for help. At that moment, there was no-one on the other side. But then my dad came round and she could help him up from the floor where he had fallen. Last night I had cut short a supper arrangement with our old German friend, Wolfgang, and hurried to my dad's home.

"Hassen is sick, Wolfie," I said. "We will have to spend the evening with him."

One look at him when I arrived made me realise my dad was really ill. He was short of breath, not able to rise from the chair where he sat beside his bed. I called my sister, the one who is a doctor, and told her he was breathless. By the time she checked him, he pretended to be fine.

"My creator, my creator," he mumbled as my sister and I tucked him into bed.

"It's only the flu, dad," I said. "Every time you feel a little sick then you talk about dying."

I smeared his cold feet with Vicks Vaporub, rubbing them until they were warm. It would help him to have a good night's sleep. I put off the bedside lamp and drew the door closed slightly so that he would be not be disturbed by all of us.

Ruschka has a cold so I have kept her home from school. "Keep indoors today," I say to her as I dress for work. I don't want your cold to get worse." She flings her arms around me. "Bye, mom. Don't worry."

I get into my car, on my way to work. Something tells me to go to the hospital first. Since my dad contracted leukaemia nearly two years ago, I have never visited him when he went to hospital for his monthly check-ups. It was a routine thing. Some days he would come back after a few hours. Other days he would stay the whole day to receive a blood transfusion. "Come and see him tonight when you get home from work," my mom had said this morning. "I will take my book and go and sit with him for the day."

But I find myself driving towards the hospital. Best to see him before work, I think. Perhaps I get home too late tonight.

I walk into the ward but his bed is empty. I ask the nurse his whereabouts. She says she will check, disappears and does not come back. But then I see her with another nurse down the corridor and approach them. I again ask after my dad. The second nurse says: "I am afraid your father has just passed away."

My body pulls stiff as a plank. Tears well up in my eyes. My voice contracts as I hear the rasping, incredulous question in my own voice: "But who is here with him?"

"Your mother has just arrived and she is with the doctor," says the nurse.

She leads me to the room where I find my mother alone, her face ashen and withdrawn. "He's gone, Beida. He's gone."

I hold her close to me as she sobs and I can hardly cry. Then my brother Adam and Zerene arrive. Then comes Julie.

My dad was alone when he died. Well, not entirely alone. There was a nurse preparing him for an X-ray when he went from this world. But not one member of the family was at his side. Julie and Adam had gone to work, knowing that my mom would soon come and sit with him. Zerene, Adam's wife, was the last one to see him alive.

The nurses escort us into a room where my father lies. He is still warm and my mom flings her arms around him, laying her head on his chest. The lips are parted and the face is glowing. He looks almost youthful in his death. All the strain is gone. Not an old grey face straining to breathe. The face appears flushed and at peace. I am happy for him. So sorry for myself. I cannot cry. I have to convince myself that I am in control.

We are caught up in the practical arrangements. My brother Sulaiman is methodical, stoical. He is on his cellphone calling those who can help with the burial arrangements. My dad died just after 11 a.m. According to the custom, we have to bury him before sunset tonight.

I have a child who must be told. She cannot stop weeping. I have to be strong for her. When they bring the body from the hospital, she is close to hysteria. She squats on the floor beside the stretcher and strokes her "oupa". She will not move, angry when a relative tells her not to upset herself.

I take the Qur'ān and settle on the bed. The only way to cope now is to recite the Arabic words that could bring some solace. It would have made my dad happy. I chant so that my daughter can be helped and so that I can too and so that my dad's spirit can soar. My brothers carry his body to a vacant room in the house where it is to be washed.

Our neighbour, Makiyah Moerat, carries in red rose petals to scatter around his face. My brothers help with the ritual ablutions and prepare him for his final resting place. The Islamic burial is simple. The body is wrapped in soft white cotton wool and white linen cloth. A white sheet covers the body as it lies on a flat metal stretcher that is used for other burials.

Mourners file past the body to say their last goodbyes. He will leave the house at 4.30 p.m. As the time draws nearer, people continue to flow in. Outside in the street, a crowd has gathered. Not everyone can fit into the house so they stand outside, as is the custom.

Sheikh Nazeem Mohammed arrives. He has risen from his sick bed to be with us. He was the religious head of our local community but also a neighbour and close friend of my father. He had been my Islamic teacher, had officiated at my wedding, the naming of my child, my divorce. He was an integral part of my father's world and his life and was an integral part of mine.

"Hassen was a man who had no enemies," he says. "If there was somebody out there who was his enemy, the problem was with that person. He was loved by all."

Minutes before the brief ceremony commences, Finance Minister Trevor Manual squeezes through the tightly packed passage and stands beside the sheikh. He brings words of sympathy from the president and the cabinet.

I know they are about to slip the body into the bier and carry it from the house and down the street. I quickly whisper to my brothers Adam and Sulaiman that they should not rush, and should give the female family members an opportunity to get onto the stoep so that we can see the body being carried away. As women, we do not get to go to the graveyard. A relative does not like the idea and blocks my mother from leaving the house.

"This is against the Sharia," he says.

My mother stops in the doorway. She does not argue. It would not be appropriate at such a sad moment. I find it so strange that she has to be stopped. How can standing on the stoep and seeing your husband of fifty-six years being carried away to his grave be unIslamic? There is nothing that suggests to the rational mind how this could be harmful or wrong.

It's a small tussle that goes unnoticed by most. My dad was a broad-minded man. He would have wanted to see his wife and daughters say their last goodbye and we are doing just that. Ruschka is sobbing next to me as the men carry the bier down Sunbury Road. I keep my eyes fixed on the dark-green embroidered cloth covering his body for as long as possible. Then they turn the corner, taking him to his final resting place, and I feel like a part of my body has been torn from my flesh, leaving a raw bleeding gap that weakens my soul.

CHAPTER TWENTY-ONE

M̲y chest is very tight. I cannot breathe. I am on my knees, my body doubled over and my forehead touching the bedspread as if I am praying. I stretch out my arms in front of me because I need to widen the chest area. It's an exercise I learnt in a yoga class I have been attending off and on. Nothing helps. It's getting worse. I have to admit defeat and accept that perhaps this is beyond self-control. I pick up the telephone and call my sister.

"You need to go to the hospital immediately," Julie says. "I will get Addy to take you."

Ruschka has left for school so I am alone. Within fifteen minutes my brother Adam arrives. I can hardly walk. I am not getting enough oxygen. He helps me down the stairs, out through the front door and into his car.

At the Wynberg Medical Clinic, he fetches a wheelchair. He pushes me through the entrance and straight to the emergency outpatient section of the hospital.

The nurse knows the routine for an asthma patient. On goes the oxygen mask across my mouth and into my arm goes a needle attached to a drip that feeds into my veins. I feel like I am fading in and out of consciousness. I am sick. I am really sick. Why have I been so stupid to leave this so long? This is a new thing that I developed last year during the 1999 elections when I was living in Johannesburg for six weeks, coordinating the election coverage for Independent Newspapers. The company doctor in Johannesburg had diagnosed me and given me a pump. I must say I have not been taking the asthma too seriously. This is the first time that I feel I cannot breathe at all.

They test my oxygen levels and place the mask back on my face.

I hold my brother's hand, suddenly feeling extremely vulnerable. I cannot understand what is happening to me. Is my body giving in? How long is this going to take?

After about three hours, the doctor makes a decision. "I cannot let you go home today," she says. "Your chest is not opening up. We will have to admit you overnight."

In a way, I feel a sense of relief. I am safe and close to help. They wheel me up into the ward, help me out of my clothes and into a hospital night-dress. All the while the drip accompanies me on a mobile pole.

The nurses raise the bed so that I can sit propped up. This helps me to breathe. Lying down is an impossibility. As soon as I try, breathing becomes more laboured.

When the night comes, my body is tired. I am so very tired of sitting up and trying to sleep. My chest remains tight. A bit easier than this morning but tight. The family visits but leaves Ruschka at home.

"She can come tomorrow when you are a little better," says my mom.

The next day, I am not much better. I am quite agitated because I am worried about being away from work. I am worried about all the undone tasks that seem terribly urgent to me as I lie here. I must see Clive, my deputy. I feel I will only be able to rest once I inform my office of what needs to be done. It's such a silly attitude, to think that one is indispensable. Not that I consciously think I am but I do have a rather over-developed sense of responsibility. So what if I am sick? They can come and ask me if they need information about specific tasks, I tell myself.

But I am not able to convince myself. I make a list in my mind of everything I was supposed to do yesterday, today and this week. I am conscious that I am being stupid yet I cannot stop myself.

When Clive walks into the ward, I can barely speak and I can see his concern. Just two weeks earlier, we had interviewed candidates for the position of my deputy. I needed somebody to help me and had needed somebody for three years now. The work pressure was too great. I had too many people I had to satisfy, too many people. Fourteen news desks making demands, some of which were unreasonable. Clive got the highest score in the interview and was the leading candidate.

As he comes towards the bed, I remember the day the company announced my appointment as parliamentary editor and the nastiness I had had to face. Here is this same man, his face full of concern, sitting next to my bed. I had put aside my personal feelings and appointed him as my deputy because I had to accept that he was the best available candidate for the job. And in the past three years, I had rather come to appreciate his open hostility. It was somehow more acceptable than the subtle vindictiveness of a small group of white men inside and outside the company.

"What can I do for you, my child?" one of the editors had said when I was about to brief him and his senior staff.

"She has gotten it all wrong this time," colleagues in the parliamentary press gallery had said when I broke the story of Mandela's secret marriage plans.

Gossip. Gossip. Gossip. Please don't tell me what is being said, I asked colleagues who felt they should tell me about the rather damaging stories being spread. I don't want to know.

"You are pure evil," said a less-than-subtle colleague when I challenged the received wisdom of the old boy's club. Clive had been there that day and at least he had had the decency to stop the man.

"You don't worry about anything," Clive says now. "Just get better."

My chest heaves as I ask him to take down a list of tasks. When I am finished, I feel such a sense of relief, knowing that I can forget about it all. He leaves the ward. I close my eyes and feel my breath slow down and my arms slump loosely at my sides, no longer stiff like branches of a tree.

I don't know who I am. I am sitting in my garden, on a low wooden chair, unaware of the grass beneath my feet. I don't know who I am. I am not sure. I have been so used to being the journalist or the activist. Now I am able to be neither.

The pumps did not help. The nebuliser helped temporarily. I just could not breathe. I am slowly realising that this cannot be a physical thing, that there is an emotional component. That I have to attend to the emotional. I resign from my job as group parliamentary editor. It is as if all my skill has left me, flown away like a bird to other shores. I feel naked, vulnerable, barely able to get through the day.

Thank God I have Ruschka to see to. She needs her food when she comes home from school this afternoon. I cannot disintegrate completely. After twelve years, I am back with therapist Ramsay Karelse.

"You are depressed," he says. "Work with me."

And I am trying to do that under this tree. I have strict instructions to let my mind break through the barriers closing it off.

"Think back and let yourself feel the emotions that you have never felt."

This morning and every morning, I think back. I take my little blue note book and write without thinking. I am following Ramsey's orders. I must just write in an unstructured way. Just let it come as it pops into my head. I recall my feelings as I have been doing for weeks now. I am remembering.

Not remembering as I recalled events that day at the TRC. Then I spoke in a numbed state, recalling but not feeling. Hanging on to the little pill beneath my tongue. I did not want to feel because I was too afraid that it would overwhelm me. And I was right. The emotions are strong. They come in waves. No, not in waves. Waves are regular, steady, predictable mostly. These come in tidal waves. Out of the blue. Unexpected. Some days and not others. I am tired of writing. I gaze at the lemon tree with its hard green lemons, unripened, tight, hard. I place the little blue book and the pencil on my chair and step into the house to make myself a cup of tea. The writing eases the anxiety but there is a heavy dullness in my brain.

I hear my father's voice on the telephone as I wait for the kettle to boil.
"Beida?"
My mind takes me to that moment when I heard his voice.
"We have a surprise for you," the men had said. "A very nice surprise," said one who was particularly nasty.

My legs give in and I go down onto the kitchen floor.
"I am so sorry, dad. I am so sorry. I am so sorry."
Am I going mad? I am on the floor. What am I sorry about? I am so sorry to hear you on the other end of the telephone. So sorry that you are enduring such indignity on my behalf. I sob and sob and sob. For the first time I unwrap the pain that engulfed my heart twenty years ago.
I lift myself from the floor and walk slowly into the bedroom so that I can rest on the bed. The tea will have to wait. An electric shock has passed through my body. It is shock lodged deep in me washing out into the universe. I am very tired yet calm. So calm.
I am beginning to understand how the mind works and am fascinated.
"Feel the pain, so that you can see it as it is, then let go of it," Ramsay says. Week after week he sees me in the consulting room at his home. "You can call me or come see me whenever you need to," he says. "Don't worry about paying me."
He knows I am not on medical aid and I am not working. I vow that as soon as I am working I will pay him back. But can I ever pay him enough for chipping away the hardened shell encasing me?
Who am I? What am I going to do?
"I definitely cannot write anymore," I say to Ramsay. "I definitely cannot organise anything. What will I do? I have a child to look after."
"First get better," says Ramsay. "Depression is an illness. You are ill. If you had a broken leg, would you step on it? No. Well, your mind is damaged and you have to give it time to heal. You cannot step on it."

It is as if I cannot take too much stimuli. The radio is too loud. I cannot look at a newspaper. I am suffering overload. The hard-drive is full and cannot carry any more information until I completely delete some of the files.

I went to school just a few weeks before turning five. I remember having to keep up, keep up, trying too hard to please. I don't want to do it anymore. To please my father.

A small group of men around me in the interrogation room. A small group insulting, swearing, pushing me beyond my limits. Pushing, hitting, threatening, beating. Shaking, shuddering in terror. My husband's intense demands. A small group of men at work who finally press all the buttons that unleash an extreme reaction to the intricate chain of circumstances determining my destiny.

Inside my mind I examine each link, digging deep within myself to find the reserves of energy I need to unhook one from the other.

I am back in the garden the next week. Who am I if I am not a journalist or an activist? Who am I? I don't know. Days pass into weeks and I do not know. I sit in silence then kneel down to slowly pull the weeds from the grass in little patches. Who am I? The answer jumps into my consciousness like an unexpected grasshopper: I am Zubeida. I am a rather nice person and I like helping other people. That's who I am. Even if I do not write one word again, I can still be me. I can still be me.

The answer is the key opening the padlock hooking the chain together. The tiredness seeps from my muscles through my fingers stuck in the grayish black soil beneath the strong cords of grass that creep across the garden. A rush of energy gushes into my body, giving me the strength to loosen the next link of the intricate chain.

Perhaps I can sell something. If I have to, I will give up my house for a while and stay with my mom and just be.

Suddenly everything seems less difficult.

I walk into my home and prepare the afternoon meal, grilling fresh fish in the oven and steaming some butternut to go with the rice I had cooked earlier. In a small pan, I braise onion, tomato, chilli and garlic because I know Ruschka loves it.

The door opens as she half falls into the house. She has this way of making her presence felt and does everything with real gusto. The schoolbag is dumped next to me in the kitchen as she wraps her arms around me, kissing my cheek. "Beidi, Beidi." It is as if she senses that I need to feel her physical strength close to me.

"How was your day, Ruschi?"

"Great. I ran around the field at school and did not get tired."

As I unearthed the shocks in me, she too has slowly been shedding her anxieties, finding a new energy that had eluded her after I left her dad.

"We are just going to concentrate on sorting ourselves out emotionally this year," I had said to her. She had taken to the task like a duck to water. Regular gym, healthy food that I had time to make and lots of talking about how we had both felt about the divorce and the problems that had followed. Gradually we had come to terms with the feelings of anger towards her dad and could cut the cords that entrapped all three of us.

As the sun sets, we allow the water to flow over our hands, our elbows, our foreheads, our feet. It is time to pray. The ritual ablution is a physical cleansing that is an integral part of the preparation for prayer. I have come to rely on these short meditations spread throughout the day in accordance with religious fiat. It brings a certain calmness to my mind and creates a ritual that binds me to my child. I do not manage the prescribed five times a day but do my best to make time in the mornings and evenings.

Islam is a combination of tried and tested practices that focus on strengthening the spirit. So do many other religious practices. I am always telling Ruschka that people of different religions are in different cars but we are all travelling the same road. It does not matter which car you are in as long as it is a vehicle moving you along that path. I find it odd that intelligent human beings are entirely comfortable with the notion of making time for intellectual development through study, playing sport or exercising for physical development but question the need to dedicate time to nurture and develop their spiritual dimension.

Seated on our colourful prayer mats in my room, she turns to me as we complete the meditation, her face glowing.

"Mom, I feel so light. I don't feel sad. I love my dad and I know he loves me."

"He loves you very much, Ruschie. He is not always able to show it."

I hold her in my arms, conscious that she has reached a state that I aspire towards as I steadily unbind the chain.

After supper, Miriam Makeba's voice tumbles down the staircase. Ruschka has slipped her CD into the music centre. I hear the words and feel the vibrations of "Pata, Pata", her famous dance song. Suddenly it is possible to twirl around with my daughter in the living room. For months now I have only been able to cope with complete silence. Every song sounded like a loud noise jangling my nerves. Now I am slowly able to engage with it in small doses.

Ruschka has started a fire in the hearth and we flop down on the comfortable chairs when we tire of dancing. I am pleased that I built this house four years ago in the yard where we grew up. For five years after the divorce, I shared my parents' home with my brother Mansoor, his wife, Kayzuran, and their children. Now they have taken over the house and I have constructed a wonderful home right next door. There is a gate between the two houses, making it possible for the children to run in and out at will. I wanted Ruschka to grow up in the community, to be able to play in the street and run into the neighbour's home. Individual, isolated living can never be for me. I wanted her to grow up with her friends and numerous cousins around her and if there is one thing that I have achieved it is that. I hope that she will go into the world strong in the knowledge that she is one part of many.

We speak about her day at school and my day at home.

"Ruschie, some company has done a survey about what South African students are doing in their spare time. They say white students spend their spare time in bars, coloured students walk around in malls and African students spend their spare time in the library."

"What am I, mom?"

"You are not one thing, Rusch."

"Then, I want to be an African student. I want to spend my free time in the library."

"You can be whatever you want to be. But mainly you are a child of the universe, of God. You are part of everybody. That is the central message of the pilgrimage to Mecca. Nobody is better than you nor are you better than anyone else. Your oupa always drummed that into our heads.

"Remember our famous Xhosa saying: Ubuntu ungamntu ngabanye abantu – a person is only a person through other people.

"With apartheid gone, you can be many many different things at the same time. You are Muslim, you are South African, you are African, you are coloured, you are of this world and of another. You have it all."

I have been reluctant to dwell on issues of race. She is at high school now and I think I can take the chance.

"Do you feel intimidated by the white children at your school?" I ask rather shamefacedly.

She looks surprised.

"No."

"You don't feel you have to be like them?"

"No, mom. They feel they want to be like me."

It's my turn to look surprised.

"To be multi-cultural is cool. It's the in thing. Didn't you know? It's real cool."

CHAPTER TWENTY-TWO

She curls up in the window seat in my study, waiting for her friends to arrive. "He is a slut, mommy. A slut. And she likes him." Ruschka is concerned about one of her friends who has a crush on a boy in the neighbourhood.

"A slut is used in reference to a woman who has low morals, Rusch," I say.

"I know that, mom, but he is a slut. There is no better word. He would like to say that he is a player but he is just a slut."

We hear our gate click open. The girls are arriving. Tasneem, Zeenat, Mishal. There are a string of them. Some afternoons, friends from school swell the numbers. Jessica, Lisa, Aqeelah.

The girls I can cope with but slowly the boys considered "dumb" a few years ago prowl the street, ring the doorbell and drape themselves over my lounge chairs.

In some ways, mothering became easier as she grew up but now suddenly the challenges are different. Hormones are dancing. Thank God I am getting better and regaining my energy for the next round of living.

"Do you want your friends over for your birthday, Rusch?"

She hesitates. Our level of sociability declined drastically last year after my dad died. Then I fell ill and could barely cope with the boisterous teenagers playing loud music in her room.

"Let's talk about it tonight, mom," she says as the chirping girls plonk kisses on my cheek. Ruschka bounds towards the cupboard to remove two thick blankets to cover their legs as they settle in to watch a movie. The school term ends next week and the daily homework regimen has already slowed down.

Ramsay has given me a collection of short poems by the Persian mystic Jelaluddin Rumi. Chilean writer Isabel Allende's *Paula* lies abandoned on the coffee table. Five or six lines of poetry are more manageable for my bruised mind. Books will have to wait. I am reading the lines of Rumi's *Quietness*.

> *Inside this new love, die.*
> *Your way begins on the other side.*
> *Become the sky.*
> *Take an axe to the prison wall.*
> *Escape.*

The axe is chopping through the wall that imprisons me.

Walk out like someone suddenly born into color.
Do it now.

I am. I am trying to.

You're covered with thick cloud.
Slide out the side. Die,
And be quiet. Quietness is the surest sign
That you've died.

I have died and live again.

Your old life was a frantic running
from silence.

Busy, busy, busy, too frightened to face my deepest emotions.

The speechless full moon
comes out now

It is shining, shining, soothing, stroking me so that my injured soul can heal. I stretch out on the couch with the poems resting on my stomach and close my eyes, listening to the happy patter of the girls coming through the wall from the adjacent room.

"Call me as soon as you leave Grassy Park," I say to her cousin Ayesha over the telephone. "I must know when you are on your way."

"Sure, Aunty Beida," says Ayesha. "Don't worry."

Ayesha was named after her grandmother and greatgrandmother. Her mother's mother was Ayesha and so was my father's mother. She is Ruschka's oldest female cousin. A petite young university student, pale with jet black hair tied up in a short pony-tail. In her spare time she is an amateur beautician, adept at the pencilling of the eyebrows, painting the lips and sweeping the hair into fashionable styles. She is treating Ruschka to a makeover. Their first stop this afternoon was the hairdresser, followed by shopping at the Claremont mall. The final stop was Ayesha's home in Grassy Park for a dress change and facial make-up.

At home, I am rather nervous. Ruschka's other mother, Mozena, has the food under control. I have baked a chocolate cake and am decorating it with a thick layer of caramel and grated chocolate. We have pushed two tables together, creating one long surface with about twenty chairs arranged around it.

Last week, when the movie ended and the girls went home, we had discussed her birthday and decided to give it a miss. Working out the logistics became too much. She has seventeen cousins, a stepsister and brothers who have other siblings. Then her friends in the neighbourhood and at school. We were not even factoring in all the uncles and aunts and the granny.

"Forget it, Ruschka. I don't think I will cope. Usually the family pops in, so let's see who comes. Next year when you are sixteen, we will have a party."

"Sure, mom."

She did not appear upset but two days previously, I had got a niggling feeling that we needed to break our cycle of mourning. I had gone into action, rounding up the younger relatives for a surprise party.

Will they get here in time before she does? I watch the back door anxiously. Her cousin Junaid is the first to step in.

"Salaam (Peace) Aunty Beida," he says.

"Salaam, Junaid," I say. "I am so glad you have got here in time."

He has run away from campus to be with us. No longer the little boy whom I carried in my arms, he has grown into a handsome young man. His slick brown hair is flicked back, exposing his forehead and soft brown eyes that speak of a sensitivity not often the forte of the male of the species.

The others slink in through the back door before 7 p.m., following my instructions meticulously.

"Don't park in front of our house. Park in Ottery Road and come down the lane next to Uncle Mansoor's house. We are going to surprise her. If you are late, it's going to be a disaster."

The smells of roast chicken, frikadels (meatballs) and sweet yellow rice waft through the room as the cousins arrive. Accompanied by her husband, my stepdaughter Leila has brought her stepsister from her mother's side who adores Ruschka. We quickly discuss logistics. Then the phone call comes.

"Aunty Beida, we are on our way," says Ayesha. "I am taking Ruschka out this evening but we are first coming to have a quick supper with you. Imraan is with us and I am bringing my friend Sultana along."

She speaks for the benefit of Ruschka who is beside her in the car. It is the signal I have been waiting for. "They'll be here any minute now. Shu! You will have to be quiet."

They squeeze tightly against the walls at the back of the room to hide

152

themselves from view. My sister-in-law Kayzuran has her finger close to the light switch.

"Is this the time to come home?" I say as Ayesha and Ruschka enter the front door. "The supper is getting cold."

"Mom, look at me. You are not looking at me."

"Wow, sweetie! Ayesha has been busy." In front of me stands my daughter, taller than I, no longer a child. Her blow-dried hair curls at the center of her back, half-way between her shoulders and her waist-line. Her lids are lined with black pencil accentuating dark-brown eyes that brim with happiness. She is wearing light-grey pants, red slip-on shoes and a dark-red cotton shirt, falling below her hips.

Down the passage we move and into the lounge that extends towards the dining room. Kayzuran flicks on the light.

"Surprise!"

She backs away from the sea of smiling faces, then laughs, a clear, light, happy laugh. "Oh mom!"

I join her other mother for supper next door at my brother's home, leaving Ruschka to bask in the love of her peers as they tuck into the mounds of food spread across the long table.

CHAPTER TWENTY-THREE

There is a lump in my throat and I blink to hold back my tears. The body will soon be carried into the hall. As usual Madiba's arrival is causing a stir. He shakes people's hands as he makes his way to the stage dressed in one of his famous floral silk shirts. Then he stands, tall, regal, the epitome of all that we have striven for. I look up at him from where I sit. He has reached the stage and stands there alone. His mouth lines droop, his eyes lose their twinkle. It is as if he stands to attention, his mind completely focused on the door as the people rise to their feet. I look to the right straight into the bright morning sunlight pouring through the open door. A row of uniformed men are silhouetted against the outline of the door-frame. Walking on either side of the draped coffin, they labour to carry the large, heavy body of Govan Mbeki into the hall for the funeral proceedings. They are mainly white men, generals of the new South African National Defence Force, arch-enemies of old, carrying a man whom they had fought against for decades.

First the one leg jutts out, then the other – stiff, single movements like sharp short kicks practised in an aerobics class. The procession pauses for a few seconds as the military man at its head salutes President Thabo Mbeki, who has come to say goodbye to his ninety-one-year-old father.

Slowly they lift the body onto a small platform erected in front of the stage. I feel my heart thud hard against my chest. The lump tightens in my throat. The tears well up in my eyes. I cry not for Oom Gov. We had said our good-byes earlier this year when I had spent a few days with him at his home in Summerstrand. He had been intensely lonely in the last months of his life, too considerate to make demands on his children. In his last days, he had desperately wanted them around him but had not been able to bring him-self to tell them. "They have many responsibilities, Beida," he had said. For support he had turned to Mamisa and her family who lived nearby, and he had received it.

No, I don't cry for him, but out of amazement and happiness to be alive to glimpse an ephemeral moment that captures the momentous change in our country. White Afrikaner military men respectfully carrying a black man to his final resting place with white and black South Africa bearing witness. Often when we speak of change, we add up the number of houses that have been built, the electricity cables that have been laid and the water provided to millions. Yet, the change in the interpersonal cannot ever be quantified in dry statistics. We have to look for these moments that tell the bigger story of change between people so long physically torn apart by law and ideology.

At the end of the service, a cavalcade of mourners line up their cars behind the military vehicle transporting the body. Mamisa and I squeeze into the back seat of a car next to Archbishop Desmond Tutu, dressed in his clerical robes. As the cortege winds its way through the streets of Kwazakhele towards the cemetery, thousands of people line the streets to say their last goodbyes to Oom Gov. Women wearing their overalls, men in worn-out sweaters and children who look as if they had gone to bed on an empty stomach the night before. All along the road, there are rows upon rows of corrugated iron shacks, a stark reminder of how the vast majority continue to live in our country. Oom Gov had left instructions that he be buried in a neglected cemetery where many who had died in the fight against apartheid lay forgotten.

In the days leading up to the funeral, local authorities and groups of local youth had been engaged in a flurry of activity to clean up and restore some respectability to the long-neglected area. In his death he remained steadfast to his life's commitment of turning our minds towards those who are most needy.

As the line of cars proceed, the mourners become aware that the archbishop is in the car passing by them. "Tutu, Tutu," they shout with delight, some peering through the car windows, others trying to push a hand into his. Their joyful reactions remind us of the past.

"These are the people who used to be part of those huge crowds when we fought apartheid," says Tutu.

"They live in the same conditions of squalor they lived in then," I say.

"We still have a long way to go. But just look at our people. They have been so patient, so generous, so willing to forgive. There are people who have so much and who complain all the time. They don't know how lucky they are. They don't understand how generous the people have been," says Tutu.

"Tutu, Tutu, Tutu." His name is passed from the lips of one mourner to another all along the road.

But for how long, for how long will this patience endure?

Members of the crowd swell the numbers at the cemetery. They are kept behind a cordon line at a considerable distance from those who have become notable politicians and dignatories. The heat overwhelms me and I feel faint. A friend grips me firmly and walks me to her car where the cool air-conditioned interior helps to revive me.

Slowly mourners weave their way past the shacks back to the university hall where they share food prepared by the Mbeki family as is the custom after a burial. Mourners are handed white cardboard trays with meat, rice, vegetables and salad. Family members return to his home for the ritual washing of the hands ceremony while parliamentarians, invited guests and ambassadors are directed to a hall in the centre of the city where they are treated to a three-course meal. Joining this group, I find myself seated at a table next to members of parliament. I look around the hall and feel ashamed. All the ostentation. Long material drapes in black, green and gold cover the walls – enough to make hundreds of flags. Numerous round tables with pristine white table cloths and delicate flower arrangements have been specially sponsored by a leading cellular telephone company. The resources go towards pandering to the fancies of those of us who are not in need.

I eat with great difficulty. The food chokes me. I cannot eat.

I think of those in the other hall a distance away in the township and the many poor and black people on the fields around them who are not fortunate to share in this meal. Why could we all not have eaten a simple meal together? Here in this hall are black and white South Africans who stand on the backs of those thousands. A combined effort won the democracy we all enjoy. A democracy that has deracialised an extreme inequality mocks me wherever I go. Those backs that hold us up can break, taking all of us with them. I close my eyes and pray: "Dear God, may those of us who have, turn every spare resource towards strengthening those on whose backs we stand. We can do it. We must do it."

I open my eyes and we have all been transformed into big fat eggs. Full yet brittle. I am Humpty Dumpty, the famous egg that flitted in and out of my early childhood. Perched comfortably on a wall built of human backs with the other eggs at my side, I survey the world of starched white serviettes, designer suits and shiny spoons forgotten in left-over mint ice cream. The wall groans in agony and buckles, flipping us through the air.

We crash onto the floor, breaking into little pieces.

> All the king's horses and all the king's men
> cannot put us together again.

Outside the hall, my friend Mamisa is waiting for me. All I want is to go to her home where I can be quiet and close to Oom Gov and his dream of a South Africa free from racial and sexual oppression and exploitation.

I am lying on her bedroom floor, resting my back. The hardness of the floor is pleasurable against my back. A relative is curling up to sleep on the bed next to her. We are all exhausted, resting after the funeral. I accept that he is at peace and the sadness in me has subsided. The lump in my throat has disappeared and the muscles in my neck are soft. I allow my mind to drift back to the previous day, when I arrived in Port Elizabeth. It was a day I will never forget for as long as I live. It looms as large as an Imax image in my mind.

The plane shudders as it lands on the runway in Port Elizabeth. The engines screech like alarmed sea gulls. With abrupt jerks, the awkward machine lumbers to a halt near the terminal buildings.

I am seated next to a young woman with whom I have had the usual inane conversation one has with people who sit next to you on these flights. We get up, gather our hand luggage and stand in the packed aisle waiting to disembark. She is of average height, with her hair tightly braided against her scalp and she exudes a pleasant self-confidence. I am here for the funeral of Govan Mbeki, I say.

"Oom Gov," she says with affection, as if to correct me. She tells me she has just been interviewed for a job as manager of Environmental Affairs at Eskom, the national electricity supplier. And has been successful. A young black woman. A manager? Environmental Affairs? The parastatal Eskom? Every single notion is strange. Every single idea a complete impossibility under apartheid. It is pleasing to observe the numerous opportunities our young democracy has created yet painfully shameful to note a deepening joblessness and ongoing poverty. We have made great strides but need to make even greater ones to achieve a social wholesomeness that we all deserve.

How old could she be?

"I am thirty today. It's my birthday."

"Happy birthday," I say.

I am so proud of her and tell her so. She smiles and says something that jolts loose the last of the hardened shells encasing my emotional memory, popping open the crucial link in the intricate chain.

"I must thank you and other older people like you for doing what you did so that we can have a different life."

157

I stop her on the tarmac. I am remembering. Other passengers stream past us. I am excited. "Please, I just have to share something with you," I say.

"It's my nephew's birthday today." It all comes pouring out. I have to speak. I have to tell her where I was on this day, 7 September, twenty-one years ago.

I am in a small room in the Sanlam Centre in Port Elizabeth, where so many had met their deaths. My mom and dad are sitting in front of me. I cannot speak. My dad pulls my scarf off my head, fearing that my ears are damaged. I speak very little. I am too terrified. There is a security policeman in the room with us.

"Your sister has had a baby boy this morning," says my mom.

It is one of the few things that registers, bringing me a little closer to the surface. I am somewhere deep down in myself, gone from this world. Pushing down as far as I can. Pushing. My parents are pulling. They work in perfect harmony. My dad distracts the policeman. My mom is able to move from the one side of the little table to the other. I am in her arms. I cannot push and she is pulling.

"Tell me what they are doing to you," she whispers in my ear.

I let go: "Mom," I whisper, "They are going to kill me."

It is the last thing I wanted to say. I had tried so hard not to speak so that they would not be hurt. I feel if they know what is happening they will be devastated. As my mom hugs me, she has the presence of mind to say: "Don't be silly. There is too much publicity on your case."

Then they are gone. I am driven back to Humansdorp to the cells where they hold me. I cannot think of my situation. I prefer to focus on the sea and the mountain to wipe away the anger I feel at myself for unduly burdening my mother. My body feels stiff like a board. It's hard to relax. I reach for the Qur'ān and open it randomly. I gaze at the page and an Arabic word pops into my conscious vision. "Junaid", meaning little fighter for truth and justice. I circle the word with my pen and smile. If only there was some way I could let my sister know that I like this name for her son.

The last of the passengers are streaming past us. We are still standing on the tarmac. The young woman is patient and allows me to speak.

"Fortunately, the next day, I saw my parents briefly again and could send the message to my sister," I say. "And every year since then, I have forgotten my nephew's birthday. Every year. My sister has to call me to remind me."

We walk towards the airport terminal and say our goodbyes. I collect my bag from the conveyor belt, walk to the door where I wait for Mamisa to fetch me. The early-morning sun shines warmly on my face. I am filled with an indescribable feeling as I see Junaid in my mind's eye, handsome, a young man who has come of age today. I hear his laughter, light and happy, reminding me of the night Australian pianist David Helfgott had hugged him and repeatedly told him: "Be kind, be kind. Be aware. Be aware. Be happy. Be happy. Why not? Why not?"

Yes. Why not?

Behind him, I see my sweet daughter, Ruschka, fifteen years old, running towards me, bright black eyes in a smiling, shining brown face, making me happier than I have ever been, with a feeling of exultation like something growing and swelling inside of me, joy, wanting to burst out of my throat in singing, out of my eyes in light, out of my heart in love and out of my soul in freedom. I reach into the brown handbag slung over my shoulder, find my mobile phone and call my sister Julie, so that I can wish Junaid happy birthday.

After 1994, ALBIE SACHS became judge of the Constitutional Court, the highest court in the land. He continues to hold this position.

ALAN BOESAK, on the eve of becoming Ambassador to the United Nations in Geneva, was imprisoned on charges of misusing anti-apartheid funds that he continues to dispute. He now works in the educational and religious sphere.

ARCHBISHOP DESMOND TUTU headed the Truth and Reconciliation Commission, retired as archbishop and is still active in public life.

CHERYL CAROLUS became South Africa's ambassador to Britain and is now head of South African tourism.

CHRISTMAS TINTO became a member of parliament in 1994 and has since retired.

ESSA MOOSA has been sworn in as Supreme Court judge.

GRAEME BLOCH stepped out of formal politics and is director of Bookeish!, the book festival set for Cape Town in 2004.

IVY KRIEL died still hoping to be compensated in some way for her son's death.

JAKES GERWEL became the director-general (chief of staff) in the office of Nelson Mandela and directs his foundation.

JOHNNY ISSEL became a member of the Western Cape Provincial Parliament. He went on to become director of a fishing company.

JULIE JAFFER works part-time as a medical doctor at the Wynberg Military Hospital. Her son, Junaid, is an actuarial science student.

MILDRED RAMAKABA-LESIEA served on the welfare committee of the Provincial Government after 1994, then became member of parliament in the National Assembly in 1998. She continues to hold this position.

MAMISA CHABULA continues to run the biggest medical practice in Motherwell, Port Elizabeth and is leading the drive to regulate traditional initiation practices.

MANSOOR JAFFER worked as communications officer at the Truth and Reconciliation Commission and is now deputy editor of Community Newspapers in Cape Town.

RUSCHKA is in Grade 11, loves road-running and soft-ball and is charity monitor at her school.

SHEIKH NAZEEM MOHAMMED died in 2000, just months after my dad's death.

TREVOR MANUEL became Trade and Industry Minister, then Finance Minister, a position he continues to hold.

VIRGINIA ENGEl became personal secretary to Nelson Mandela towards the end of his tenure as president and now heads the clothing workers union welfare trust.

ZACKIE ACHMAT has become the key AIDS activist in the country.

ZOLI MALINDI did not enter formal politics in 1994. He stayed on in Guguletu where he ages gracefully.

ZORA MEHLOMAKHULU refused a position in politics and stayed on in Langa to organise the unemployed. She died unexpectedly of an asthma in 2001.

SPYKER VAN WYK died before 1994.

FRANS MOSTERT left the security police and works with a private security company in Gauteng. He did not take up the offer of telling the truth in exchange for amnesty.

EPILOGUE

"Our deepest fear is not that we are inadequate.
Our deepest fear is that we are powerful beyond measure.
It is our light, not our darkness, that frightens us.
We ask ourselves, who am I to be brilliant, gorgeous, talented and fabulous?
Actually, who are you not to be?
You are a child of God.
Your playing small doesn't serve the world.
There's nothing enlightened about shrinking so that other people won't
   feel insecure around you.
We were born to make manifest the glory of God that is within us.
It's not just in some of us; it's in everyone.
And as we let our own light shine, we unconsciously
Give other people permission to do the same.
As we are liberated from our own fear,
Our presence automatically liberates others."

Source unknown, widely attributed to NELSON MANDELA

THANK YOU
❧

Ten years ago, Albie Sachs asked me to write about my life experiences. I started and in the process loosened the nightmares associated with my detention. I had to stop in order to cope with holding my daily life together. "Don't worry, the time will come when you will be ready to write," he said.

I remained committed to the idea and was only able to give expression to it when I sent a sample of my writing to Njabulo Ndebele late in 2001. "What is this doing in your desk drawer?" he said. He passed it on to Amina Mama of the African Gender Institute (AGI) who encouraged me to apply for their three-month writers fellowship. With additional support from my brothers and friends Joseph C. Reid, Mary Kay Blakely and Barbara Rodgers, I spent three wonderful months at All Africa House at the University of Cape Town writing continuously. The one and only time the story unleashed in me a torrent of emotion, Ginny Volbrecht of the AGI was there to support me. She held me as I feared I was falling apart and we agreed to call Dr Ramsay Karelse who as usual provided advice that helped me gain the strength to carry on.

My mom and sister, Julie, generously cared for Ruschka during the week while I wrote and from time to time packed me some home-cooked meals that made a great change to the take-away foods in Rondebosch.

My niece Ayesha Jaffer and her friend Sultana Mapker spent many hours scouring through micro-fiche at the National Library to check dates and detail of historical events. Albie Sachs guided me through the process from beginning to end, urging me to not make media issues the centre of this book but my own transformation. My life as a journalist belongs to another book. Friends and family members who read through the early drafts provided many useful insights. My sister, mom and brother Mansoor provided valuable checks. Virginia Engel, Pregs Govender, Zubeida Brey, Antjie Krog, Mary Kay Blakely, Phyllis Wender, Karin Cronje and Imām Gassan Solomon gave of their time to read the manuscript and comment.

My hiking friend, Terrence Smith and his company Target Projects, generously provided secretarial support in the person of Neli Sangotsha.

Both George Hallett and Rashid Lombard were characteristically helpful in giving photographic advice, complementing the indispensable work done by my editor, Di Paice. Dr Charles Villa-Vicencio of The Institute for Justice and Reconciliation (IJR) where I work as a political analyst gave me the time to put the finishing touches to the manuscript.

Through the months of work, my daughter, Ruschka, displayed a sense of patience without which I would have had much greater difficulty in giving birth to "Our Generation". Instead it slid out as easily as a fish slithering smoothly through the deep ocean.

May 2003